# MACKINTOSH FURNITURE

## TECHNIQUES & SHOP DRAWINGS
## FOR 30 DESIGNS

## MICHAEL CROW

**POPULAR WOODWORKING BOOKS**

CINCINNATI, OHIO

popularwoodworking.com

# MACKINTOSH FURNITURE

## TECHNIQUES & SHOP DRAWINGS FOR 30 DESIGNS

MICHAEL CROW

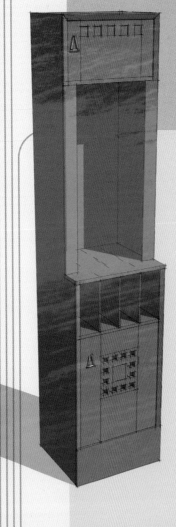

# CONTENTS

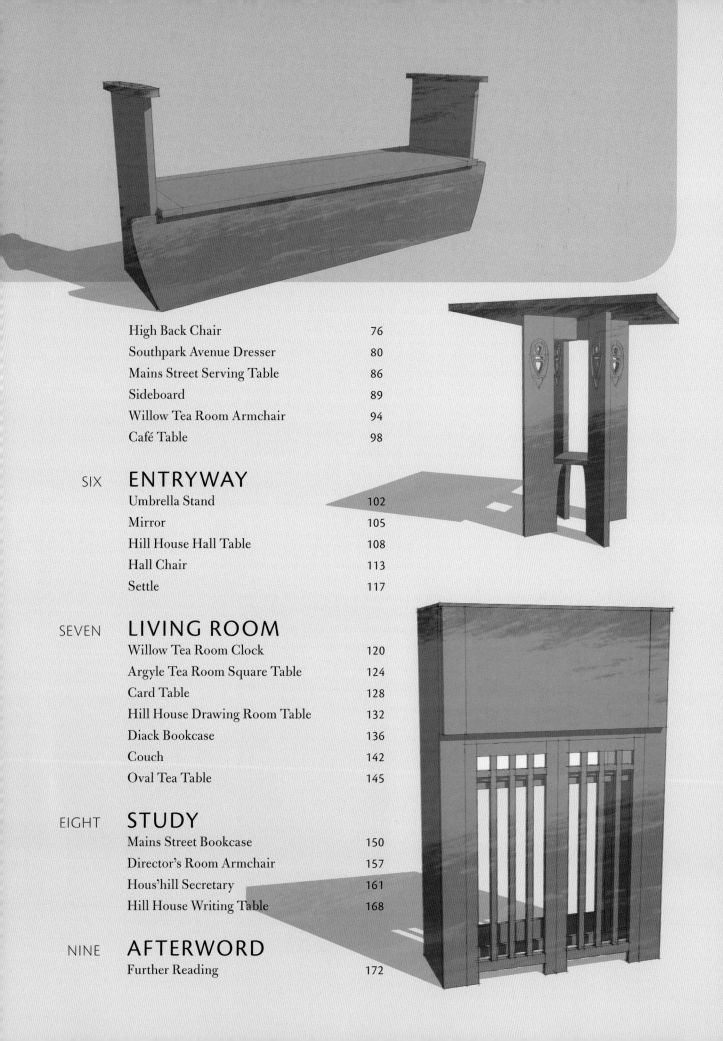

# ONE

# INTRODUCTION

## CHARLES RENNIE MACKINTOSH (1868-1928)

IN MANY WAYS, THE FATE of the sofa Charles Rennie Mackintosh designed for the Ladies' Common Room of the Glasgow School of Art echoes the reputation of Mackintosh himself, enjoying a moment of popularity before fading into obscurity and finally re-emerging into unexpected recognition. After a short life serving its intended purposes, the sofa was shuffled from the Ladies' Common Room, working its way through the school until it was accidentally set on fire and discarded. Salvaged by a student, it found new life for a time as a rack for a sculler's oars. How much more neglect it might have survived isn't clear, but it sold at auction for $24,060 in 2013.

Although he was never set on fire, Mackintosh's career follows a similar trajectory to the sofa he designed. He enjoyed an early period of success, influencing a generation of European designers, only to have his commissions dry up before dying of cancer in obscure poverty. After his death, Modernists looking to create an origin story for their movement reclaimed him as an iconoclastic hero. A subsequent interest in Art Nouveau prompted later critics to consider his ability as designer and artist working in that style. When a chair designed for Hous'hill sold at auction for the unprecedented sum of $14,400 in 1975 (which would be approximately $64,000 today), the architect's popularity began to skyrocket. Today he is firmly established as one of the leading European architects of the late 19th and early 20th centuries. His designs have become a commodity, appearing on everything from mugs, to jewelry, to typefaces, and even paper napkins, a proliferating "Mockintosh" available in any museum's gift shop with a Mackintosh piece in its collection and endemic to Glasgow, the city of his birth and site of his greatest work.

Mackintosh (then "McIntosh" – he changed the spelling of his name in 1893) was born on 7 June 1868, the fourth of William and Margaret's 11 children. The family lived in a small top-floor flat near the city's cathedral until Mackintosh was six when the family moved to a newly built home in the residential suburb of Dennistoun. There Mackintosh enjoyed gardening in the plot his father tended. This early interest in nature found literal expression in Mackintosh's botanical sketches and permeated much of his design work in more stylized ways. Likely dyslexic, Mackin-

In the late 19th century, Glasgow was an industrial capital, with commercial ties to much of the world. Wealth, an ambitious public works program and a skilled labor pool made it a rich environment for an ambitious architect like Mackintosh.

tosh failed to distinguish himself as a student in any subject other than drawing while enrolled at Reid's Public School and later at Allan Glen's Institution.

Mackintosh began his five-year apprenticeship in 1884, working in the office of John Hutchison. Although there was an effort underway during this period to formalize the training of architects via an academic curriculum, apprenticeship was still the standard practice in Glasgow at the time. Mackintosh supplemented his practical education with evening classes at the Glasgow School of Art. He studied drawing, painting, modeling and design in addition to classes on architecture and building. These classes mark the beginning of Mackintosh's long-term association with the School of Art, a relationship culminating in his design of the school's new building and Mackintosh's most important public work. He distinguished himself as a student there, winning multiple prizes and drawing the attention of the school's new Director, Francis (Fra) Newbery. The progressive Newbery transformed the school, expanding the scope of its programs and bringing prominent scholars to lecture at the school, including John Ruskin. Newbery and Mackintosh became lifelong friends, and the director helped launch the architect's career. Perhaps most profoundly, he also introduced Mackintosh to his future wife, Margaret Macdonald.

After completing his apprenticeship in 1889, Mackintosh joined the firm of Honeyman and Keppie, working as a draftsman for £5 a month (that would be around $661 today). John Honeyman had been a prominent figure in Glasgow architecture, although his reputation was beginning to wane by the time Mackintosh joined the firm. The Beaux Arts-trained John Keppie became Honeyman's partner in 1888, bringing a roster of clients and youthful ambition to the firm. As a draftsman at Honeyman and Keppie, Mackintosh would have spent much of his time on menial tasks, surveying sites and tracing drawings, with much less time

Charles Rennie Mackintosh photographed around 1903.

to actually design, first assisting one partner or another with detail work before gradually taking on larger parts of a job. The firm's cashbooks show a steady increase in Mackintosh's salary over the years – £16 per month in 1899 ($2,110) – suggesting greater contributions to the practice's design work. In this same period he took on freelance design work, ranging from furniture (including his only designs intended for mass production), to interior decorating, to domestic renovations.

Glasgow during the last part of the 19th century provided a rich ground for an aspiring architect. At this time, the city was one of the richest in the world, a center for trade and manufacturing, with global commercial ties. Commerce entailed the exchange of ideas as well as goods, providing a designer with the latest from the U.S., continental Europe and newly opened Japan. The city's wealth also supported an aggressive and forward-thinking public works program while its industrial base fostered a class of workers experienced with

The Eighth Exhibition of the Vienna Secession served as a honeymoon for the Mackintoshes. They exhibited there in 1902 with Herbert and Frances MacNair.

The couple collaborated on the design of their flat at 120 Mains Street, creating a restful, minimalist interior. Their work encompassed some furniture design, including the table for the dining room.

construction, manufacturing and shipbuilding. It is in this environment of rich patrons, vibrant creative culture, ample building opportunity and skilled tradespeople that Mackintosh began his career. Through a combination of factors both personal and historical, he was only partially able to take advantage of this opportunity.

Mackintosh seems to have resented Keppie, regarding him as an unoriginal architect more concerned with material success than creativity in design, creating a strained relationship in the office. That must have been further tested when Mackintosh passed over Keppie's sister, Jessie, in favor of Margaret Macdonald. Fra Newbery had noted an affinity between the work of Mackintosh and Herbert MacNair, another draftsman at Honeyman and Keppie, and that of Margaret and Frances Macdonald and suggested they collaborate. The meeting proved to be rewarding both creatively and personally. Working in painting, graphic arts, metal and furniture, the "Spook School" (as they were called because of their work featuring ethereal, stylized human forms at the 1896 Arts and Crafts exhibition) were the heart of the Glasgow art scene for a time in the 1890s. In 1899, Herbert married Frances. Mackintosh married Margaret in 1900. Mackintosh and his wife would continue to collaborate

throughout their careers, though to what degree continues to be debated by scholars (the debate is not merely academic – attribution drives commercial valuation, and Mackintosh commands more value today).

However fraught Keppie and Mackintosh's personal relationship might have been, it didn't immediately hurt Mackintosh's standing in the firm. He designed four important public commissions in the late 1890s, including the Martyrs' Public School and the eastern wing of the Glasgow School of Art. Construction of the School bookends the peak of Mackintosh's career, bracketing the period that saw his most impressive domestic (Hill House, 1904), commercial (Willow Tea Rooms, 1903) and public (the west wing of the School of Art, 1909) commissions as well as exhibitions in Milan, Moscow and Vienna.

Mackintosh's exhibitions and his subsequent design for Fritz Wärndorfer's music room (1902) solidified his reputation on the continent. The music room, especially, had a profound effect on Austrian and German designers over the next decade. His critical reception at home was less noteworthy and the impact on his commercial prospects were non-existent. Although he became partner in 1901, Mackintosh received no major commissions from new clients after 1905. Conversely, Keppie successfully leveraged his professional network and string of official positions to bring new business into the partnership. At times difficult to work with, Mackintosh was by temperament ill equipped for the glad-handing required to build new business. Instead, he spent his creative energy entering architectural competitions but to no avail. His shares in the profits of the partnership trace this decline in sharp relief. In 1908, he earned £918 ($114k), in 1909 £204 ($25,300), and in 1910 £77 ($9,330).

A depressed Mackintosh turned increasingly to drink. Former office mates reported that his lunch often lasted from 1 until 4:45. Even the patient Keppie could tolerate only so much. When Mackintosh failed to produce the drawings for an important competition, the two agreed to dissolve the partnership. Mackintosh made a halfhearted attempt to establish his own firm, but with no current or prospective work, he quickly closed.

Seeking what was to have been a temporary change of scenery, the Mackintoshes left Glasgow for the village of Walberswick on the Suffolk coast. Recuperating there from a severe bout of pneumonia, Mackintosh took up watercolors. His solitary behavior and habit of evening walks along the beach caused suspicion in the insular village. He was arrested as a German spy and only convinced authorities of his innocence with some effort. Following the incident, the couple settled in London.

Mackintosh once again tried to establish an architectural practice, but with no established clients in the wartime city, his prospects weren't good. With the exception of his last design for a Cranston tea room and the renovation of Wenman Joseph Bassett-Lowke's Northampton home, most of his few commissions during this period are minor and of little note. During this time, Mackintosh supplemented his limited architectural income as a freelance designer of textiles. Surviving examples of these designs tend to heavily stylized flowers and foliage and often show a high degree of geometric abstraction, reflecting both post-impressionism and Viennese influence. Working for firms across Great Britain, including Sefton's in Belfast and Liberty & Foxton in London, Mackintosh produced textile designs for £5 ($475)–£20 ($1,900) a piece. That Mackintosh could earn £200 ($9,390) in a year at such a rate (as he did in 1920) speaks to his ability as a graphic

Mackintosh had a gift for dividing larger spaces with semi-permeable boundaries. Here in the Willow Tea Room, an open partition creates intimate spaces within the larger room. Vertical dividers separate the stairway without isolating it.

Mackintosh had control of the overall design of the Scottish section of the 1902 Turin Exhibition as well as collaborating with Margaret on the "Rose Boudoir."

designer. While in London, Mackintosh continued to exhibit his work: at the International Society of Sculptors, Painters and Gravers in 1916 and 1917, and at the British Arts & Crafts Exhibition in 1920, although he does not seem to have garnered much attention.

The end of the war suggested the possibility of additional architectural work. Mackintosh executed a handful of modest commissions, including the re-design of the guest bedroom and furniture at Derngate for W.J. Bassett-Lowke. In 1920 he was poised to take up projects that could have re-launched his career in England. A series of commissions for artists' studios near Mackintosh's home in Chelsea promised steady work. His ambitious plans for a block of studios and studio flats for the Arts League of Service would have matched many of his larger public works in Glasgow. With the exception of one modest studio, these plans never materialized, stalling out due to a lack of funding. The failure of the Arts League scheme proved the final blow to Mackintosh's career as an architect. He received no commissions after the age of 52, when he turned his attention to painting full time.

In 1923 the Mackintoshes traveled to France for a rest cure for Margaret's asthma. As with the couple's earlier Walberswick holiday, what was originally intended as a temporary stay became more permanent. In France, they lived in genteel poverty on Margaret's modest private income and whatever savings they had left, moving from village to village near the border with Spain where Mackintosh turned his architect's hand and artist's eye to producing a series of remarkable watercolors. He produced these landscapes by first observing a place intently then painting in place, refusing to sketch or paint from memory. Unlike his architectural sketches or botanical paintings, which were generally documental in nature, these landscapes played with reality as Mackintosh transposed and transformed elements of the environment to suit his vision. Mackintosh had planned an exhibition of this new work once he had finished 50 paintings, but that plan, like so many before, did not come to fruition. Cancer of the throat and tongue prompted his return to London for treatment. Surgery and radium treatments proved ineffective and Mackintosh died on 10 December 1928.

In the decades following his death, critical interpretation of Mackintosh's life and work has encompassed as many contradictions as his designs do. His best work juxtaposed a series of opposites – the modern and past, light and dark, form and void, graceful curves and regimented geometries. He has been seen as a pioneer of Modernism, as a Victorian of his time, as an able collaborator, as a fiercely independent designer. That so many interpretations can exist simultaneously suggests something unknowable at the core of his personality. Moreover there's validity to each of these interpretations, for Mackintosh was an eclectic, finding inspiration where he could and transforming it into a unique expression of singular vision. Critics will continue to interpret Mackintosh's life and work, but a central assumption of each of these sometimes-conflicting readings is a central agreement that Mackintosh produced an important, influential body of work, one that continues to inspire today just as it did over a century ago.

A period postcard shows the kissing bridge in Walberswick. During the height of wartime paranoia, Mackintosh was arrested as a spy in the small village.

Longtime patron of Mackintosh, Catherine Cranston ran a string of successful tea rooms in Glasgow. She favored old-fashioned clothing, dressing in a style of the mid-century.

## MAJOR COMMISSIONS

Ranging in scope from single rooms to major public buildings, Mackintosh's commissions ran the gamut from mundane to spectacular. The following section highlights some of his most important work, from small projects, like the renovations at Derngate, to multi-year efforts like the Glasgow School of Art.

### The Cranston Tea Rooms

It can be hard for a modern audience to grasp the impact of tea rooms in Glaswegian culture in the last part of the 19th century. In a time when the temperance movement had great influence, they provided a socially acceptable place to eat, including ladies-only rooms as well as recreational areas for reading and billiards. Tea rooms offered an expanding middle class not just a place to eat, but the chance to escape into a fantasy space one cup of tea at a time. Recognizing that strong interior design would attract customers, the eccentric Catherine Cranston built a chain of the city's most successful shops. She sought out avant-garde designers to create her tea rooms. Beginning in 1896 and continuing for the next two decades, Mackintosh designed a series of tea rooms for her, first painting murals in the George Walton-designed Buchanan

The color and shape of the Willow Tea Room's exterior provided a striking contrast to the other buildings on the street, drawing welcome attention.

The rear room of the Willow Tea Room.

The Willow Tea Room's Room de Luxe featured opulent art-glass doors and silver-painted furniture with purple velvet upholstery.

Street Tea Room, then designing furniture (see the card table on page 128) and light fixtures in the Argyle Street tea rooms in 1897. At the Ingram Tea Room, he began a series of renovations in 1900. The project would occupy him intermittently over the next 12 years. In 1903 Mackintosh had free reign to design the façade and complete interiors of the Willow Tea Room on Sauciehall Street. With its sculpted white front standing in sharp contrast with other buildings on the street, the façade opened onto one of Mackintosh's great interiors, an Art Nouveau design that skillfully negotiated the tension between public and private spaces inherent in the demands of tea room design. Depending on its intended audience, the furniture in the Willow Tea Rooms ranged from delicate to sturdy (see the arm chair on page 94). Cranston remained Mackintosh's steadfast patron, and his work for her from 1896-1917 shows the full range of his interests as a designer, moving from the Arts & Crafts and Art Nouveau of his early designs for Argyll Street and the Willow Tea Rooms to the Orientalist fantasy of the Chinese Room, and the jazzy, geometric design of the Dugout.

## Hill House

Follow the River Clyde northwest out of Glasgow about 30 miles, and you come to the suburban town of Helensburgh. Accessible from the city by rail at the turn of the 20th century, it provided a retreat for those eager to – and able to afford to – escape the city. The publisher Walter Blackie joined this group, bought a plot of land about a mile north of the river with expansive views of the countryside and commissioned Mackintosh in 1902 to design a home. The architect took

Mackintosh interpreted traditional Scottish forms to design the Hill House. The tower stair used here was influenced by Baronial architecture.

Photographed here looking west to the main entrance, the Hill House entrance hall also served as additional living and dining space when needed.

A barreled ceiling isolates the sleeping area from the rest of the Hill House's main bedroom. The headboard integrates night stands similar in design to those used in the Blue Bedroom at Hous'hill.

great pains to understand the family's needs and produced his domestic masterpiece, Hill House.

Coming in under budget at a cost of £6,200 in 1902 ($800,000), Mackintosh exceeded expectations. With its main axis running east to west to take best advantage of the view, the house is a study in opposites. The asymmetrical grouping of visual masses, irregular fenestration and stair tower evoke Scottish Baronial architecture (a favorite source of inspiration for Mackintosh) as does its roughcast surface, but the style is rendered in a modern, almost abstract fashion. The austere exterior conceals a comfortable interior, where every detail, from the shape of the rooms to the design of the carpets has been considered for effect. The master bedroom shows a strong Art Nouveau influence, but the drawing room intermixes organic and geometric forms (like the latticed base of the table on page 132). The hall is more rigidly linear; the play of negative and positive space and minimalist decoration calls to mind Mackintosh's interest in Japanese design. With its slab legs and pierced cutouts, the hall table (see page 108) is perfectly suited for this space.

## Hous'hill

Mackintosh didn't design only tea rooms for Catherine Cranston. In 1904, he redecorated several rooms at her home, Hous'hill, at a cost of £1,422 ($182,000). The commission included two bedrooms, the Blue Bedroom for Cranston and her husband, and the White Bedroom for guests. From inlays to latticework, the square

Mackintosh moves away from painted furniture to natural wood tones in Hous'hill's Blue Bedroom. Visible on the right is the chimney cupboard.

provides the dominant theme in these rooms as geometric forms abound, completing the transition from Art Nouveau seen at the Hill House. Finished in natural colors, the oak furniture of the Blue Bedroom featured the use of leaded glass and bright tiles (see the washstand on page 62, chimney cupboard on page 67 and secretary on page 161). The furniture in the White Bedroom was painted white – the last of Mackintosh's furniture designs to be painted white, ending the use of a technique first implemented at Westdel around 1898.

Hous'hill's White Bedroom was the last of Mackintosh's white interiors. The black chairs provide a strong visual counterpoint to the room's white-painted furniture.

Because its construction encompassed so much of Mackintosh's career, you can read the history of his interests as an architect in the exterior of the Glasgow School of Art. Part of the first phase, the east face detailed here shows how he repurposed Scottish Baronial forms in the design.

## Glasgow School of Art

Today the Glasgow School of Art is regarded as Mackintosh's greatest work, but its original critical reception was less unanimous. Built in two stages (south wing 1899, north wing 1909), the building shows the full range of Mackintosh's interest as an architect. Carefully considered solutions for the needs of its intended audience were combined with disparate inspirations into a singular expression. The east elevation of the school incorporates elements from Maybole Castle, which Mackintosh had sketched in 1895, while the rational geometry of the southern elevation shows an affinity for the work of the Vienna Secessionists. And with its evocation of the natural world and dark wood, the building's most impressive space, the library, calls to mind the work of Arts & Crafts designers. What might have been simple pastiche is transformed by the architect into an expression uniquely Mackintosh. This ability to combine sometimes conflicting impulses into a single whole might have been his greatest gift; it's certainly one that makes it easier for critics to find divergent readings in the same body of work.

Most of the furniture designed for the library is institutional in nature, but Mackintosh designed pieces for the director's office and board room that would also serve in other professional or domestic settings. The armchair designed for the director's room (see page 157) is one such piece.

## Derngate

In 1916 J.W. Bassett-Lowke commissioned Mackintosh to renovate his Northampton townhome at 78 Derngate. Bassett-Lowke was an educated consumer with a strong interest in modern design. It may have been the challenge of working for a well-informed client that pushed Mackintosh into new territory, for Derngate marks a departure from his earlier work. Structural modifications to the home included relocating the staircase to divide the living room from the dining room. The back of the house was extended a few feet to add room in the kitchen and dining room. Balconies were created for the master and guest bedrooms. Mackintosh's living room design called for black paint on the walls relieved by a vibrant geometric stencil dominated by yellow triangles. The sparse furnishings feature a lattice-back settle. Upstairs, the bedroom designs were more restful but still used vibrant colors and geometric stencils. The furniture is mahogany and often inlaid with mother-of-pearl and Erinoid, an early plastic. The geometric impulse running through Mackintosh's furniture finds its logical end in minimalist forms such as the guest bedroom dressing table (see page 50) and hanging mirror (see page 105).

## FURNITURE DESIGN

With the exception of his work for Guthrie & Wells in the mid-1890s, Mackintosh designed his furniture with a specific client (and often a specific location within a site) in mind – part of the totality of effect he tried to achieve. It's this thoughtfulness and minute attention to detail, more than a set of specific characteristics, that distinguishes his furniture design. One piece might be in the Arts & Crafts style, another in Art Nouveau and yet another anticipates the Bauhaus. With its graceful lines and attenuated form, the high back chair designed for the Ingram Street Tea Room (see page 76) shows Mackintosh as practitioner of Art Nouveau, as do the stylized flowers and art glass of the Mains Street Bookcase (page 150). Just a few short years later, his furniture tends toward geometric abstraction, the slab sides and cutouts of the Hill House Hall Table and the precise grid of the Willow Tea Room clock showing an affinity for the Vienna Secession. And his last furniture – designed for Bassett-Lowke – carries minimalism to an extreme. It is problematic (if tempting) though, to describe the evolution of his furniture design as a progression towards a

Modern minimalism, for more traditional forms coexist with modern at times in the same works. The Glasgow School of Art has been cited as the impetus of Modernism, but the library evokes the medieval monastery. The organic and the geometric intermingle in the furniture of the Hill House drawing room. Even the Derngate furniture, arguably Mackintosh's most Modern, shows the same concern for craft and the character of wood as the Arts & Crafts movement. Regardless of the style he worked in or what historical sources he might be building on, Mackintosh's furniture designs share a purity of line, consideration of form and void, and a thoughtful effect of the piece on the whole of the work. It's these traits that made his furniture striking when it was made and help explain its lasting appeal today.

This photo of the Willow Tea Room's Smoking Room provides the only record of the oval table. Both table and chair show Mackintosh's evolving interest in geometric abstraction. The cutouts and slab sides share an affinity with some Vienna Secession designs.

Reinterpreting the traditional gossip's chair, Mackintosh designed coopered hall chairs for Windyhill.

Mackintosh produced a number of variations on the basic form of the writing table featured in the master bedroom at Hill House – tables with slab legs set at 45° to the aprons.

## Construction

It may be ironic that someone so versed, as was Mackintosh, in the work of John Ruskin and the Arts & Crafts movement seemed to consider how his designs were actually built as an afterthought. Painted furniture might unify an interior (his white rooms) or visually punctuate a space (the Hill House writing desk), and that effect is more important than joinery or grain, which are

obscured under filler and enamel. Even when wood isn't concealed under six coats of paint, it isn't always assembled with the best techniques – screws feature heavily in the construction of the round taboret (see page 26). To be fair, Mackintosh seems to push the material available to him to its limits in the interest of design, and the Tea Room furniture, at least, had to be built in relatively large numbers at a price that wouldn't bankrupt the client or the cabinetmaker.

In most cases the cabinetmakers were either Francis Smith or Alexander Martin. These large shops (Francis Smith employed 90 people) produced the bulk of Mackintosh's furniture. As firms in one of the world's industrial capitals, they likely would have had access to modern machine shops and assembled furniture built from a variety woods (including oak, pine, cypress and mahogany) using a combination of machine and manual techniques. Their output was serviceable, but not especially noteworthy. It is tempting to wonder what Mackintosh furniture might have been like had the designs been executed more thoughtfully. Here the architect brothers Charles and Henry Greene serve as a possible analogue. Like Mackintosh, the Greenes designed furniture for the homes they designed, but in the Hall brothers, they found cabinetmakers willing and able to build to exacting standards. The results are exquisite. The furniture built for Bassett-Lowke hints at what might have

To understand the full impact of Mackintosh's spare interiors, it is helpful to compare them to a typical Victorian room. To someone used to patterned wallpaper, heavy curtains and cluttered space, his bright, airy rooms and graceful furniture would have been quite surprising.

been achieved had Mackintosh found his own Hall brothers. It's not clear who was responsible for the execution of all of these designs. German prisoners on the Isle of Man constructed at least some of them. It's possible Heals, who made the Derngate carpets, or Bassett-Lowke's own factory built some of the pieces. Whoever the maker, the pieces feature mahogany instead of oak and well-executed veneer and inlay work. Too, they show more attention to the figure and nature of wood, matching the skilled design with equally skilled construction.

## Prices

Honeyman and Keppie kept detailed job books for their projects. These provide a wealth of detail about the firm's commissions, including how much the furniture and buildings cost. I've included that information where available. It's not immediately clear how these costs equate to modern U. S. currency, so I've provided the U. S. dollar equivalents to those job book rates. Such conversions require calculating both exchange rates over a century of inflation. I'm grateful I didn't have to make those calculations. Instead, I relied on the calculators at measuringworth.com. Where required, I converted shillings and pence into their decimal equivalents using the calculator at gwydir.demon.co.uk/jo/units/money.htm. Note that these values are approximate, and the dollar equivalents are current for 2014.

## ABOUT THE DRAWINGS

In his roughly 35-year career as an architect, Mackintosh produced hundreds of furniture designs in styles ranging from Arts & Crafts, to Art Nouveau to Modern. In selecting the pieces to include here, I've chosen from the full span of Mackintosh's career while trying to include furniture suitable for all around the home. I've also tried to select pieces that can be built with a modestly equipped workshop.

The drawings are based on measurements extrapolated from known dimensions using catalog and auction photos as well as Mackintosh's original architectural drawings. With dimensions in hand, I then created three-dimensional models of the pieces before generating the 2D views and parts lists presented here. Such an approach carries with it the risk of error, and it also requires some guesswork where internal details aren't documented in the photographic record. In instances where

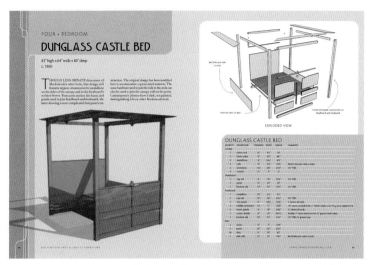

The renderings and drawings in this book are based on measurements extrapolated from known dimensions using catalog and auction photos as well as Mackintosh's original architectural drawings.

I haven't been able to view internal details, I've relied on standard furniture construction techniques to fill in the blanks. Furniture built using these drawings and the parts lists should honor the spirit of the originals even if the work does not replicate them exactly.

# TWO

# TOOLS & TECHNIQUES

ENTIRE BOOKS HAVE been written on tools and techniques for building furniture – indeed, books have been written on single joints – so this chapter does not pretend to encyclopedic completeness. Rather the information presented here is intended to give the beginning woodworker a minimum of information required to build the furniture presented in later chapters. Note, too, that you can often accomplish the same end using different methods depending on your tools, time and inclination. One woodworker might prefer to chop mortises by hand and another to rout or drill them. You can even avoid the joint altogether, substituting dowels. If you have doubts about how to cut a joint, practice on scrap before sawing into your project wood.

Following this chapter are two step-by-step projects. These projects provide the opportunity to apply the techniques outlined here while building useful pieces of furniture. For the beginning woodworker, they provide a stepping stone before tackling the independent work of interpreting the measured drawings and deciding on a building sequence on his or her own. Even if you don't build these projects, reading the processes they document will be useful as you consider how to use the tools and techniques covered here to build other Mackintosh furniture.

## TOOLS

Award-winning cabinetmaker and educator Gary Rogowski has observed that you could build anything with a band saw, router and chisel. This may be a slight exaggeration (keeping that chisel sharp, for one thing, is a skill unto itself and requires some equipment), but it emphasizes an important point. You don't need every tool or machine under the sun to build a piece of furniture. The pieces illustrated here can be built in a modest shop. Do your research before you buy, and use the techniques and tools you're comfortable with. You will need to be able to dimension stock, cut joinery, clamp pieces for assembly and prepare surfaces for finishing. Don't forget safety equipment, either. Protect your eyes, your ears and your lungs.

Many of the pieces featured in this collection can be built with surfaced lumber since they use only ¾" stock, but other pieces require different thicknesses. Buying rough lumber gives you greater control over your material as well. Jack, jointer and smoothing planes allow you to true rough stock by hand, but most woodworkers save time by using powered jointers and planers. In the small shop, a combo machine will save space but at the cost of time spent changing between functions.

A table saw is at the center of many workshops because it allows for ripping and crosscutting wood to size, and can be used to cut joinery, including dados, rabbets, grooves and tenons. While you can build without it, it does simplify many operations. A coping saw, band saw or jigsaw allows you to cut curves.

With the right bits, the router can cut tenons, dovetails, rabbets, dados and grooves. It also profiles edges. Guided by a template or bearing, the router can also be used to duplicate parts using patterns, an extremely useful capability for multiples of identical parts.

## MATERIALS
If your desire is to hew closely to the originals when reproducing this furniture, the original wood and finish is included in the individual descriptions where it was known. Oak predominates (as it does in much of the furniture of the era), but pine and mahogany are also common.

Wood selection can make or break a project, so it pays to take your time at the lumberyard. Avoid twisted, cupped, bowed or otherwise warped boards then select to match for grain and color. Buy enough material to allow for mistakes and for choosing the right wood for a given part. Let stock acclimate in the shop before use because solid wood will expand and contract with changes in humidity and temperature.

When it comes time to cut parts, keep your options open: Don't make a cut until you need to

and leave yourself slack when you can. When beginning a project, the impulse is often to cut all parts at once, but even the best cutlist and most careful measurements may yield variation between plan and part. Working with subassemblies simplifies work and minimizes risk. Try to cut similar parts at the same time so minor variations in tool setup don't lead to variations in the size of the parts. If a part's fit relies on how other parts come together – a drawer front in its opening, for example – grief can be avoided if you measure the actual distance between those parts instead of relying on the plan.

Because it is the most visible part of the completed project, use the best boards from your stack for the top. If you are finish-planing by hand, it can be useful to orient boards so the grain runs in the same direction, but otherwise arrange boards to yield the most attractive top. Generally the goal is to produce a top that looks as much like a single board as possible. There is no need to alternate the direction of growth rings or to rip and re-glue wide boards to control movement. Often, fewer boards used in a glue-up produce more attractive results, but boards of similar width will look better together than a wide board together with smaller boards.

Rails and stiles look their best when grain runs along them. They'll also tend to stay straight over the passage of time. Avoid using stock with the arcing lines of cathedral grain to make these parts. In the same way straight-grained wood can emphasize a straight piece, curved grain can complement a curved piece. And when building a row of drawers, cutting drawer fronts from a single board produces a uniform look.

## PATTERN ROUTING
Many of the designs featured here include multiples of identical parts. These can be cut individually, but for more than one or two pieces, it is more efficient to prepare a pattern and use it to guide a router fit with a pattern-routing bit. Wood, plywood, MDF or hardboard of appropriate size can be used to create the pattern. Any flaws in the pattern will be replicated in the final parts, so take pains to make a perfect pattern. Consider

A pattern bit has a bearing that follows your pattern to allow for perfect multiples.

The pattern is traced on the workpiece and roughed out on the band saw.

Guided by a bearing, the flush-cut bit follows the contours of the pattern.

completing a test run with the pattern before using project lumber.

Use the completed pattern to trace the part on the wood then rough out the part, leaving no more than ⅛" of material outside your layout lines. Once all blanks are rough cut, affix the pattern to the wood. If the design of the part allows it, the template can be built with toggle clamps. Otherwise, double-sided tape can be used, or if part of the piece won't show in the finished project, a couple of screws will hold the pattern in place. The bit's bearing will follow the contours of the pattern, trimming the rough blank to finished size.

## JOINERY

While Mackintosh designs move from Arts & Crafts to Modern, most pieces are simply built, relying on a few basic joints, including mortise-and-tenon, dados, rabbets and lap joints.

The mortise-and-tenon recurs through these pieces, joining table and chair legs to stretchers and aprons, and rails to stiles. It is a straightforward joint to cut by hand or using machines. Remove wood at the end of a piece to form a tongue sized to fit in a hole cut in the mating piece. Care should be taken when cutting this joint to ensure a firm fit between the mating parts.

It is easier to cut a tenon to fit a mortise than the reverse. Begin by marking out the location of the mortise. If cutting the mortise by hand, a marking knife or cutting gauge will help keep the edges of the joint neat. The depth of the mortise should account for the full length of the tenon and a little extra for excess glue. You can drill out most of the waste, then pare the edges of the mortise, but a dedicated mortising chisel makes quicker work of them.

There are a number of ways to cut a mortise using power tools. A hollow-chisel mortiser drills a square hole, and by moving the workpiece along the axis of the joint, a mortise of any length can be created. A router, guided by a template or a straightedge

Position the mortise chisel toward the center of the marked joint and hammer it in.

Pry the waste free and continue chopping toward your layout lines on either end of the mortise

The finished mortise is ready for assembly.

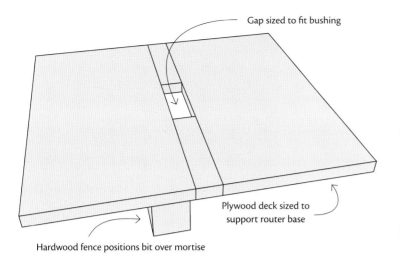

Gap sized to fit bushing

Plywood deck sized to
support router base

Hardwood fence positions bit over mortise

## MORTISE ROUTER JIG

The router's template bushing rides in the jig to cut a mortise of a specific size.

The cutting gauge is set to the length of the tenon and passed around the workpiece.

Define the shoulders.

With the shoulders defined, cut the cheeks

guide cuts clean walls, but the round ends it leaves will need to be squared or the tenon rounded to fit.

If cutting a tenon by hand, mark the joint, cut around the piece to establish the shoulder line, then cut the cheeks. A similar approach can be taken when cutting the tenon with power tools. Cut the shoulder line on the table saw using the miter gauge or sliding table, then cut the cheeks using a tenoning jig. A band saw can cut the cheeks if the piece being tenoned is too long for the table saw. Passing the piece over a dado stack will also work, as will a straight bit in a router table.

However it's cut, a tenon should fit its mortise snugly without being forced. Shave a tight tenon with a rasp, block plane or scraper, taking care to remove an even amount from either side of the tenon and to avoid tapering its thickness.

A rabbet is a groove cut into the edge of a board. Cases are often rabbeted to accept a back, and door frames and the hanging mirror (page 105) can be rabbeted to accept glass. The joint can be cut in several ways either by hand or power

tool. A shoulder plane or rabbeting plane is used to cut the joint by hand. It can be cut in a single pass on the table saw using a dado stack, or in two passes with a regular blade, one to make a vertical cut, the other a horizontal cut. A router equipped with a straight bit or rabbeting bit can cut the joint as well. When using a straight bit, the router must be guided either with an edge

With the fence set to match the length of the tenon, the blade is set to the depth of the shoulder and the workpiece passed over the blade to define the shoulders.

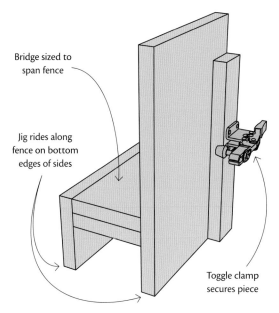

Bridge sized to
span fence

Jig rides along
fence on bottom
edges of sides

Toggle clamp
secures piece

**TABLE SAW TENON JIG**

If the tenon is too long to safely use the table saw tenoning jig, the cheeks can be removed with a band saw.

guide or straightedge clamped in position. The bearing on a rabbeting bit allows you to rout the rabbet freehand. Care must be taken at either end of the cut to avoid blowing out grain and to avoid unintentionally continuing the rabbet around the board. It's better to stop a little short and clean the cut with a chisel than to go too far.

A dado is a groove cut perpendicular to the grain of a board. Often this simple joint is used to join shelves to case sides or dividers to case top and bottom. With a bit the diameter of the desired dado chucked in the router, it's an easy joint to cut. Simply mark the board, set the bit to desired depth of cut and rout away the waste. A straightedge clamped across the joint can be used to guide the router, but this router jig eliminates the risk of wandering away from a single straight edge because its two rails capture the router. Note that due to metric to imperial conversions and manufacturing variations, the nominal thickness of plywood may diverge from its actual thickness, so a nominal ¾" panel might be thinner than stated. Try placing that panel in a ¾" dado, and you end up with an unsightly situation. Instead, rabbet the edge to bring the thickness to ½" and use a ½" bit to cut the dado.

The lap joint allows two pieces to cross in the same plane. It is often used where table stretchers cross and to produce the lattice recurring through Mackintosh designs. To cut the joint by hand, begin by marking the intersection on opposite faces of the crossing pieces. Saw halfway through each piece along those layout lines to define the shoulders of the joint, and chisel the waste free. Pare or rout the bottom of the joint smooth.

Position the fence on a case piece where you've marked for dados and clamp the jig.

## LATTICEWORK

Many of Mackintosh's designs show a careful use of negative and positive space – he often uses absence of material as ornament. This effect is accomplished through the use of pierced cutouts (usually square, but sometimes organic as well) and through latticework. Grids appear on the horizontal (e.g. the hall table on page 108) and vertical (e.g. the dresser on page 80) planes of these designs.

Two techniques are used to accomplish the lattice effect. The first relies on mortise-and-tenon joinery, the second on lap joints. The former relies on a series of evenly spaced mortise-and-tenon joints to create the grid. It is more labor intensive to produce than the alternative and appears where lap joints might leave unsightly edges. A good example of this is the single-width lattice flanking both sides of the clock on page 120. Although less forgiving because flaws in fit aren't hidden behind

A rabbeting bit features a bearing that allows you to rout rabbets freehand.

the shoulders of the joints, the lap-jointed grid requires less effort to produce. Individual joints can be cut by hand, but you can also gang cut the joint by clamping pieces together and plowing dados across them. A similar effect is created by first dadoing a wide board, then ripping and planing it into individual parts.

## ASSEMBLY

Dry-fitting, where the pieces of the project are assembled without glue and clamped to verify the final fit of all parts, goes a long way to ensuring piece of mind when assembling a project. Gather all parts and a sufficient number of clamps (and cauls to protect the wood from being marred by clamps). Decide on a sequence for assembly then put the piece together. Smaller pieces will come together easily, but larger projects are better managed in subassemblies. For example, you might assemble the ends of the table, wait for them to dry and then connect the ends with the front and back aprons. If there is difficulty with anything coming together, refine the joints until they fit.

Having rehearsed final assembly, it will go more smoothly. Hot hide glue is one option for fastening parts, as is liquid hide glue. Hide glue is reversible when treated with heat and moisture – a convenient feature should the piece ever need to be repaired. PVA, or yellow, wood glue is more commonly used today. Apply a thin layer to both surfaces of the joints (an acid brush is helpful here), fit them together then tighten your clamps.

Before the glue has a chance to set, check case goods (and drawers) for square by measuring the diagonals. If the diagonals are the same length, the piece is square. If they don't match, a clamp across the longer diagonal or a few blows with a wood mallet should bring things into square. Leave the clamps on long enough to allow the glue to cure (anywhere from a few hours to overnight, depending on the glue). If you've pre-finished the piece, you can remove your painter's tape and put your completed project in its new home. If you are assembling before applying finish coats, double-check to make sure you've cleaned up any squeeze-out because it will show under a finish. Wiping the piece with mineral spirits should show any problems.

## DRAWER CONSTRUCTION

One common way to build a drawer is to use half-blind dovetails at the front and through dovetails at the back to join the drawer box together, with

Mackintosh latticework relies on lap joints or mortises and tenons to join horizontal and vertical members. Both techniques are used in the Hill House square table.

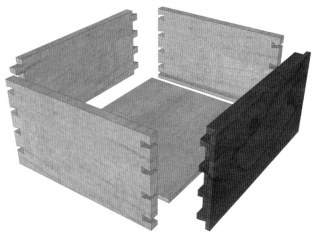

Typical dovetailed drawer construction has the front joined to the sides with half-blind dovetails and full dovetails at the back. The drawer bottom rests in grooves, and if solid wood is used for the bottom, the back of the drawer is cut flush with the top face of the bottom so it can expand and contract.

the drawer bottom captured in grooves. It makes for a strong drawer because the dovetails provide mechanical resistance to forces acting on the drawer. If the thought of cutting dovetails doesn't appeal, there are other ways to join a drawer. Pinned or locking rabbets will also work, and with an applied front, the box can also be assembled using box joints. Plywood drawer bottoms can be glued in grooves in the sides, front and back of the drawer. A solid-wood bottom, on the other hand, should be captured in the sides and front of the drawer and left to expand toward the back of the drawer, which should be cut so that it ends flush with the top of the drawer bottom.

For the drawer pulls, cut a mortise all the way through the drawer front and square the corners. If you're building multiple drawers, a pattern will expedite this step.

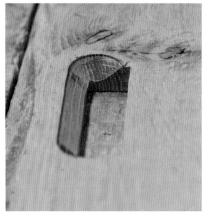

Chamfer the back of cutout's top edge. This forms the pull's grip.

If the drawer face is applied as a false front to a drawer box, the box will provide a back for the pull. Otherwise, apply a backing to the opening by gluing or tacking it in place. Your choice of material can make the opening stand out. The Washstand from the Blue Bedroom has metal backing plates painted purple, providing a bright splash of color on the drawer faces.

## Cutout Drawer Pull

A variety of period hardware in metal or wood will suit many of the designs captured here, but one common pull used in these designs – they feature prominently in the washstand (page 62) for example – requires no hardware. Instead, the drawer front is cut and shaped to form an inset pull. The pull is a simple beveled cutout in the drawer front. Either a backing panel or drawer front (if applying false fronts to an assembled box) covers the inside edge of the cutout. Begin by making the rectangular cutout in the drawer front, then, using a chamfer bit in the router or a sharp chisel, bevel the top inside edge of the cutout to form a pull. If the drawer front is integral to the drawer, cut a shallow rabbet around the inside edges of the opening and cut a backing panel to fit.

Clockwise from upper left: staple gun, jute webbing, tack hammer, pliers, gooseneck webbing stretcher, fabric shears.

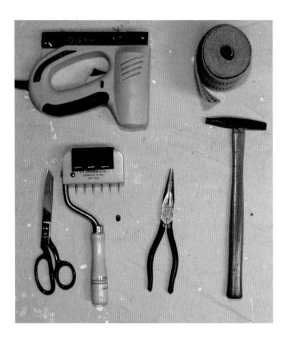

## FINISHING

The finishes used in Mackintosh's designs are as varied as the designs themselves, ranging from dark stains and ebonized effects to colored stains (like the green built-in cabinets in use in some Hill House rooms) and paint (often white, but also black and silver).

A good finish begins with good surface preparation. If sanding, begin with a low enough grit to easily remove milling marks, then work up through the grits, stopping at #180 or #220, then vacuum the work or blow it off with compressed air to remove all dust. You can also plane and scrape your parts smooth using a smoothing plane and card scraper. Surfaced stock can be sharp where two edges meet, so break all edges with #220-grit sandpaper or a light pass with a block plane.

I like to pre-finish my parts when I can, because it helps minimize drips and runs. Using blue painter's tape, I tape joints then apply my finish. During glue-up, I then tape surfaces at risk of glue squeeze-out. If you choose to assemble your work then apply your finish, pay particular attention to where glue has squeezed out during assembly because any residual glue will show under a finish coat.

## UPHOLSTERY

Mackintosh furniture uses a wide range of upholstery techniques, from rush seating to fully upholstered frames and spring seats. While some of those techniques may be better left to a professional, the slip-seat cushion featured in the dining chair, Director's Room armchair and Willow Tea Room armchair requires little specialized tooling or skills. Sized to allow some room for layers of fabric along all edges, a plywood or hardwood frame forms the foundation of the seat. Jute webbing is

Jute webbing is woven across the seat frame.

Polyurethane foam is cut to size to form the cushion.

Batting is stretched over the foam.

Muslin is wrapped over the foam and stapled to the bottom of the frame.

Show fabric is wrapped over
the cushion and stapled to
the frame.

then woven across the frame opening, stretched tight and stapled or tacked in place. For a single seat, the webbing can be stretched with a large pair of pliers, but a webbing stretcher is a worthwhile investment for more than a couple of chairs. The webbing supports a polyurethane foam cushion, which is wrapped in batting. A muslin cover is then stapled over the cushion to shape it and to hold it in place. With the cushion shaped and the muslin in place, apply the show fabric and attach it to the chair.

## RESOURCES

### Hardware
A web search will yield a staggering variety of sources for hardware. The list below contains those I've used and recommend.

**Craftsman Hardware**
www.craftsmanhardware.com
509.766.4322

**Horton Brasses**
www.horton-brasses.com
1.800.754.9127

**Lee Valley**
www.leevalley.com
1.800.871.8158

**Rejuvenation**
www.rejuvenation.com
1.888.401.1900

**Rockler**
www.rockler.com
1.800.279.4441

### Makers
**Cassina**
www.cassina.com

**Bruce Hamilton**
www.brucehamilton.co.uk

**Kevin Rodel**
www.kevinrodel.com

# MACKINTOSH IN THE ROUND

## BUILDING A TABORET
28" high x 26" wide x 26" deep

MACKINTOSH DESIGNED a number of tables on the same theme – a round top supported by slatted legs featuring square cutouts – with a number of finishes, including ebonized oak and metallic silver paint. Because he produced many versions of this basic design, it suggests multiple avenues for adapting the table as built here for your own use. Scale it up to seat more people for a distinctive dining table or shrink it down for a bedside table.

This example in oak from the billiard room of the Willow Tea Room has four slatted legs joined with mitered aprons and crossing stretchers. With its 26"-diameter top, this Mackintosh taboret makes for a larger end table or an intimate dining table for two. Regardless of use, its combination of attractive form and simple construction makes it a good starting place for building in the Mackintosh style. Pocket-hole screws, dowels or

loose tenons join the aprons to the legs, while the stretchers are screwed to the legs through plugged holes.

Final finish will determine your wood selection. The original features a dark finish on oak. I chose to follow suit, emphasizing the design's Arts & Crafts roots by building in quartersawn white oak and using a traditional fumed finish to top things off. If you prefer to paint, poplar provides a good foundation. Build and finish to suit your taste knowing the design's strong lines make it at home in a range of settings.

Begin by gluing up a slightly oversized blank for the top (about 27" square will suffice) then turn your attention to the leg pattern. It's possible to produce the 12 square cutouts by carefully drilling and cutting each individual square, but it's far easier to pattern rout the legs to final shape. Prepare the pattern by first ripping and crosscutting a board to length and width. Then, using the drawings as a guide, lay out the position of the three square cutouts. Complete the pattern by cutting out the squares; if you've prepared a cutout pattern, drill clearance holes for your jigsaw, then trim close (between ⅛" and 1/16") to your layout lines. Finally, affix the cutout

# PATTERN FOR A PATTERN

Careful drilling, sawing and chiseling will produce a neat square cutout, but that work grows tedious quickly. Instead, produce a cutout pattern and use it to shape all of the cutouts on your master pattern. You can drill and chisel that cutout pattern, but it's less effort to rip and crosscut some scrap stock to produce a perfect square cutout. Begin by ripping a strip the width of your square from the center of the board. Crosscut that center strip and cut a spacer block the length of the cutout. Glue the four pieces of the pattern together, using the spacer block between the center pieces. Once the glue dries, use the cutout pattern to rout each cutout in the leg pattern.

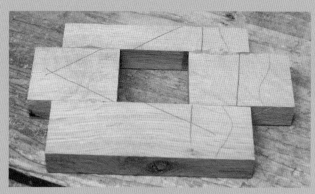

Rip and crosscut a piece of scrap to frame a square. After glue-up, it can be used to position the cutouts in the leg pattern.

The cutout pattern is screwed to the leg pattern and the cutouts routed to shape. The corners of the cutouts in the leg pattern don't need to be squared.

Finished pattern.

pattern over your hole and trim each cutout to final size using a flush-trim bit in your router.

With the leg pattern complete, you're ready to produce the slatted legs. Rip and crosscut the legs to final size, rough out the cutouts, then use your pattern to rout them to final shape, taking special care at the corners to avoid burning the wood.

While it's tempting to leave the corners radiused as the router bit left them, a square corner leaves a much neater impression. Square each corner with a sharp chisel, paring from both faces to avoid blowing out wood on one side of the leg.

The aprons join the legs at a 45° angle, and your choice of joinery determines how you'll treat the ends. If you are equipped to produce pocket hole, loose tenon or dowel joints, you can miter the apron ends to final size, then produce your joinery. If you're using integral tenons to join the aprons to the legs, you'll need to cut the aprons longer to leave material for your tenons. Because I was using pocket-hole screws, I trimmed the aprons to final size at the miter saw and drilled my pocket holes using a basic jig. If you're using pocket holes, remember to offset your holes on either end of your aprons to avoid screws running into each other when joining aprons to legs. The miter complicates the joint, so you might need to experiment before finding the right settings. Practice on some scrap before drilling your apron stock.

There are a number of ways to produce a round tabletop; I chose to rout out the top using

The sharp corners of the cutout are a small detail, but they have a surprisingly large impact on the effect of the piece. Pare one side straight, then move to the next to form a sharp corner. Work from both sides of the leg to avoid blowing out on either face.

A simple jig guides the router to cut a perfect circle. Make several passes, taking special care as you come close to finishing the cut.

a basic circle-cutting jig – a length of scrap ¼" plywood wide enough to accommodate the plunge base of the router and longer than the 13" radius of the top. Polycarbonate or acrylic plate can also be used and has the advantage of transparency, making it easy to mount the router to the jig and see where the bit is cutting. After attaching the jig to the router, mark a pilot hole in the jig, measuring the length of the radius from the inside edge of the bit. After drilling the pilot hole, drill another pilot hole at the center of the bottom of your table blank. Once the router base has been screwed to the table blank, the router will pivot along the top, cutting a circle as you plunge the bit into the wood. Limit the depth of your cut and take multiple passes to avoid breaking your bit or tearing out the edge of the top. Remember not to cut into your benchtop as you cut to final depth.

With the top and base parts cut to size, it's time to sand or plane your parts. I knocked off machine marks with a smoothing plane and sanded to #220, working my way from coarse to finer grits. Because I'd planed first, sanding went quickly. With all your parts smoothed, you're ready to assemble.

Begin by joining the aprons to legs. A block mitered and cut to the aprons' ½" setback simplifies positioning the aprons consistently. Clamp a leg and the block in place, wedge the apron underneath the block and screw the apron end to the leg.

Like the aprons, the stretchers are screwed to the legs, with a single screw joining both stretchers to the legs at either end. Mark the location for a pilot hole in either end of a stretcher, clamp the upper stretcher pair in place on the leg, and drill through the first stretcher and leg into the second stretcher, taking care not to drill through the second stretcher. After drilling pilot holes, you'll

A mitered block clamped to the leg positions the apron for screwing and also prevents the apron from moving as the screw drives into the leg.

Clearance holes are drilled in the ends of two of the stretchers.

After the stretchers are screwed to the legs, the holes are plugged. Trimmed flush, the plugs blend in with the grain of the stretchers.

# A FUMED FINISH

Fuming with ammonia is a traditional Arts & Crafts finishing technique. When exposed to a concentrated ammonia solution (approximately 25% NH₃ by weight), the tannins in white oak cause the wood to darken, yielding a rich, warm color that penetrates the surface. Depending on the intended use of the piece, different topcoats can be applied to provide different effects. Boiled linseed oil is easy to apply. Shellac offers additional protection and – depending on the shellac – can provide another layer of color. Polyurethane provides greater protection than oil or shellac.

To minimize the safety risks associated with ammonia, be sure to wear proper eye protection, long sleeves, chemical-resistant gloves and a respirator with appropriate chemical cartridges.

While smaller pieces can be placed in airtight containers for fuming, larger pieces will need to be tented in plastic. Your tent does not need to be elaborate (to fume the taboret, I draped plastic sheeting over a sawhorse and weighted it down). The wide surface area and resistance to ammonia's corrosive effects make glass pie pans useful containers for fuming. Place the piece in the tent, put in a pie pan or two and pour ammonia into them.

How long you need to fume the wood for a desired color will vary because the darkening effect of ammonia depends on a number of factors including ambient temperature, tannin levels and length of exposure. Place some project offcuts in the tent along with your finished piece to gauge color. In its unfinished state, fumed oak takes on a greenish cast; to reveal the true color of the project, remove one of your scrap pieces and apply a finish coat. Once you have a color that appeals, remove the piece from the tent. Note that you will need to freshen your ammonia after about 48 hours.

Your fuming tent doesn't have to be fancy – plastic sheeting works nicely.

Fumed white oak darkens and takes on a greenish cast. Try some different finishes on fumed scraps to find your preferred finish.

need to drill clearance holes for the screw heads at the ends of two of the four stretchers. These clearance holes should match the diameter of a plug cutter or dowel stock (I used trim head screws sunk in ¼" clearance holes and a corresponding ¼" plug cutter). Screw the upper stretchers in place and then install the lower stretchers and cover the screw holes with plugs. After cutting and sanding the plugs flush, the holes are hardly noticeable.

The top can be joined to the base with wooden cleats, buttons or metal tabletop fasteners. Whatever method is used should allow the top to shift with seasonal wood movement. Attach cleats or fasteners to the base, position the base on the top, mark the screw locations, and drill pilot holes in the top.

If you want to follow the original as closely as possible, you'll want to use a finishing schedule that combines a stain for color and varnish for protection. I opted to fume the table with ammonia to darken the oak, followed by an application of oil and wax. Had I intended the table for heavy use, I would have applied a topcoat of polyurethane instead of wax. To produce a dark finish, I fumed the table for about 48 hours before applying three coats of boiled linseed oil. I applied oil generously with a rag, wet-sanding with #320-grit paper and wiping off excess oil after about 30 minutes. I let each coat dry overnight before applying a subsequent coat. After my last coat had dried, I applied a coat of dark paste wax following the manufacturer's instructions. While it provides only modest additional protection, the paste wax covers any slight imperfections.

Stretchers screwed to legs
through pocket holes

Top attached to base with
hardware or cleats

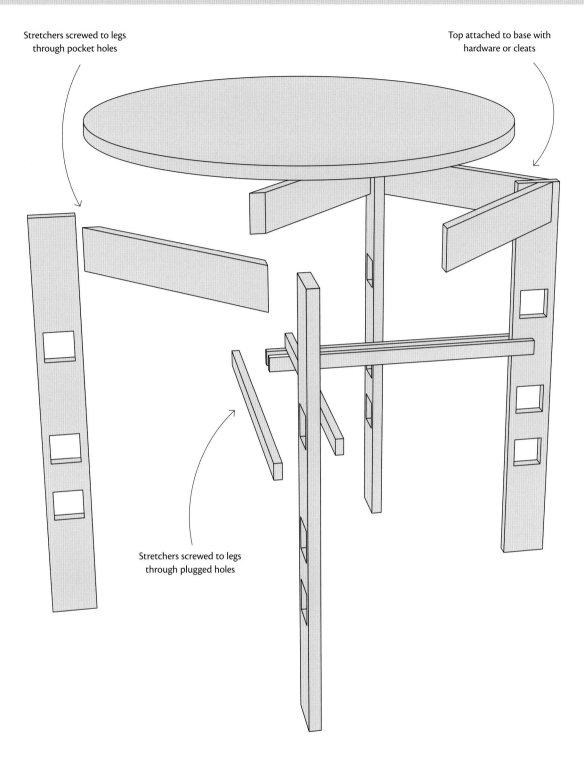

Stretchers screwed to legs
through plugged holes

**EXPLODED VIEW**

# TABORET

| QUANTITY | DESCRIPTION | THICKNESS | WIDTH | LENGTH |
|---|---|---|---|---|
| 4 | Aprons | ¾" | 2¾" | 14⁵⁄₁₆" |
| 4 | Legs | ¾" | 3" | 27¼" |
| 4 | Stretchers | ½" | 1" | 19" |
| 1 | Top | ¾" | 26"-dia. | |

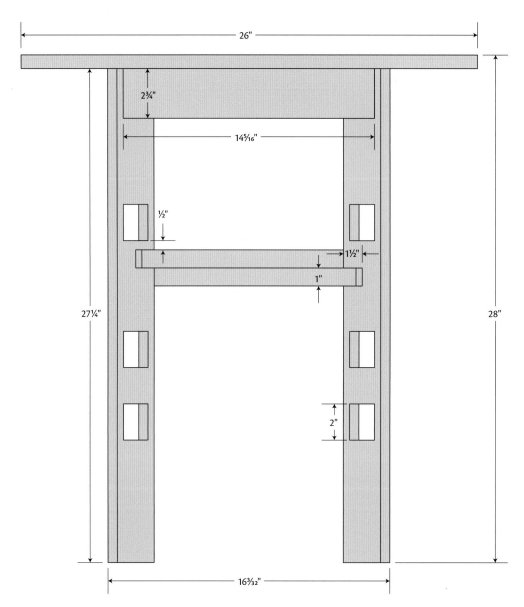

**PROFILE**

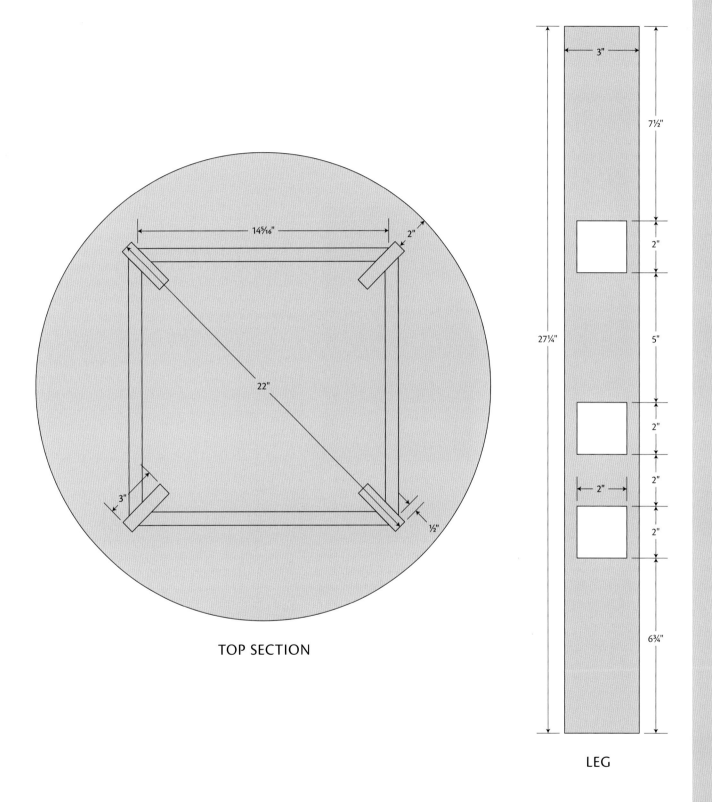

**TOP SECTION**

**LEG**

# BEDSIDE COMPANION

## BUILDING A MACKINTOSH NIGHTSTAND
28" high x 18" wide x 12" deep
(1900)

ORIGINALLY DESIGNED for Mackintosh's Mains Street residence, this side table incorporates a surprising variety of useful techniques in its construction, decoration and finishing despite its small size. Building the table provides a useful introduction to the mortise-and-tenon and dovetail joints, pattern-routing, applied moulding and painting. Two copies of the table flanked a cheval mirror in Mackintosh's bedroom, but it would serve well at the side of a bed or anywhere else a compact table is needed.

Four slatted legs support a beveled top over a single drawer, with an applied flower stem and inlaid petals decorating the front legs. Construction is straightforward, with mortise-and-tenon joinery predominating and dovetails joining the drawer sides to the front and back. This reproduction features two minor changes to the original design, eliminating the curves on the front stretcher and substituting inset colored glass for the carved and painted petals. However, the techniques and process outlined here could be used to

create a more strict reproduction if desired. Following the original, this build features a painted finish, but it would look good in a dark-finished oak or cherry as well. Because I intended to use paint for my final finish, I chose poplar. It is readily available, easy to work and provides a great foundation for paint.

Construction begins with the top. If you have access to wide lumber, you may be able to cut the top from a single piece. Otherwise, glue up a blank a bit oversized and rip and crosscut to final size after your glue has dried. The top's wide bevel can be cut on the table saw with an auxiliary fence supporting the top's edge as it passes over an angled blade, but it is also easy to bevel by hand. First mark the bevels on the bottom and edges, then plane the bevel to the desired angle, beginning with a jack plane and finishing things up with a smoothing plane.

Because they are simple rectangles, the parts of the base are easy to cut to size. Rip and crosscut as needed, then mark and cut the mortises and tenons using your preferred method. Now is a

Use a marking gauge to lay out the width and depth of the bevel.

A handplane makes quick work of the beveled top. Beginning at the ends to minimize tear out (spelching), plane until you reach your layout lines. Then move to the sides.

good time to drill the top drawer guides to accept the screws that join the base and top. Drill these toward either end of the guides, sizing the hole larger than the threads of your screws to allow the top to expand and contract with changes in humidity. With the foundation of the base complete, you can turn your attention to completing the floral detail on the front legs. The decoration comprises two elements: an applied stem and inset petals.

The original version of the table features a simple petal shape carved into the wood then painted a rosy purple to match other accents in the Mains Street bedroom. You can use a chisel and router to carve these petal shapes or pattern-rout them with an appropriate bit and router. I took a different approach, using a pattern to rout a petal-shaped piercing in the wood, then glazing it with purple stained glass. The pattern begins as a board cut the same width as the leg and long enough to clamp to the leg with enough clearance to rout freely. After preparing the blank, lay out the petal, then drill, saw and file it to final shape. Then use the pattern to lay out the design on the legs. Remember to flip the petal over when marking and routing the opposite leg to ensure the design is mirrored on the legs. If you are carving the cutout, clamp the pattern in place, then use a straight bit with a bottom-mounted bearing to rout the recess in the leg. If you are cutting out the petal, rough it out, then clamp the pattern in place and rout it to its final shape with a pattern-routing bit. Once the cutouts are complete, switch to a ¼" rabbeting bit and cut a ½" deep rabbet around the cutout in the back of the leg. I used

Lay out the pattern in a piece of plywood or scrap.

Use the pattern to mark the cutout on your project wood.

After marking the cutout, remove the bulk of the waste with a drill or jigsaw.

Clamp the pattern to the leg blank so that it will guide a pattern-routing bit.

Rout the cutout to final shape using a pattern bit.

Use a ¼" rabbeting bit to cut a ½"-deep rabbet around the back of the cutout to receive the glass insert.

a glasscutter and nips to cut the glass infill to fit inside the rabbet. If you aren't comfortable cutting glass, you can substitute acrylic and cut it with a jigsaw or band saw.

After making the petal cutouts, cut the stems. While these parts can be cut from a single piece on the band saw, I simplified construction (at the cost of a visible seam) by making each stem in two parts, ripping the straight section on the table saw and completing the curved portion on the band saw. After cutting the stems, I rounded their faces using a block plane and sandpaper. Before gluing the stems to the legs, sand the legs to #220 grit. Apply a thin layer of glue to the straight section of stem and then clamp it in place. When the glue has dried, glue the curved section in place. You may need to ease the transition between the two pieces of stem, sanding until they blend. Once the stems are installed, you're ready to assemble the base.

The irregular curves of the stem ends are best shaped by hand. The waste provides a convenient handle during shaping and is later removed.

After shaping the stem end, glue it in place so that its outside edge is flush with the edge of the leg.

Assembly is more manageable in stages, with the front and back glued up into subassemblies before being joined by the aprons, lower stretchers and drawer guides. Dry-fit your parts, apply glue, assemble and clamp. Once the front and back are dry, test-fit the sides to them then glue and clamp, verifying the top of the base is square by measuring the diagonals.

While the base dries, turn your attention to the drawer. I used half-blind dovetails at the front and through dovetails at the back to form the box, but pinned or locking rabbets or locking miters would also work. Whichever technique you choose, keep the box square to ensure it's easy to open and close the drawer. When building a small, shallow drawer, I like to maximize drawer depth by rabbeting the bottom of the drawer and gluing in a plywood bottom. After fitting the drawer, the table is ready for surface preparation and finishing.

Whether sanding or planing, take special care that the sides are flush with the front and back. Remove any sanding dust if needed and apply your finish. I brushed on a coat of primer then three coats of white acrylic paint, sanding between coats.

After finishing the base and top, there are just a few final details to complete the table: Install the glass petals (or paint the petal-shaped recesses if you're following the original closely) and drawer pull, and attach the top. To install the glass accents, apply a light bead of silicon caulk to the petal rabbets and gently press the petals home. Let the caulk dry per manufacturer directions and remove any squeeze-out and clean the glass front and back. While the caulk is drying, you can install the drawer pull. There's a wide range of "Mackintosh"-style hardware, but none of it is especially accurate. The original table featured a simple drop pull in a silver finish, and I followed suit, drilling the drawer front and screwing it in place. The last step in building the table is to attach the top to the base. Place the top top-down and center the base on it. Mark the location of your screw holes and drill shallow pilot holes, then screw the top down. Slide the drawer home and your table is ready for use.

Clamp the drawer down and rabbet the bottom, cutting to final depth in a couple of passes.

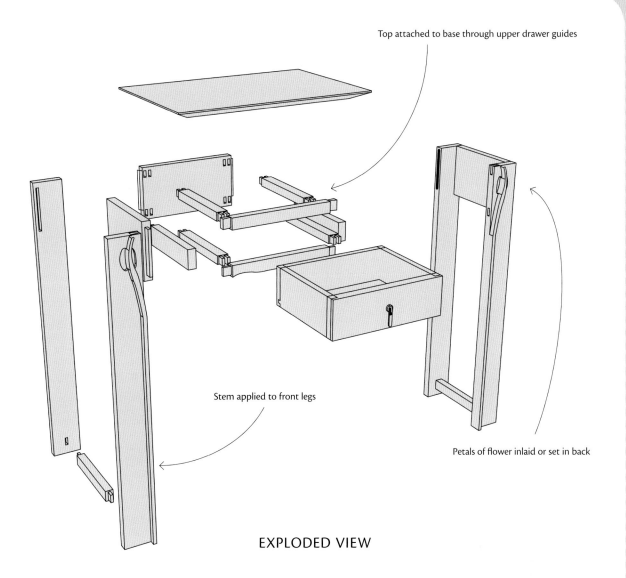

Top attached to base through upper drawer guides

Stem applied to front legs

Petals of flower inlaid or set in back

**EXPLODED VIEW**

# NIGHTSTAND

| QUANTITY | DESCRIPTION | THICKNESS | WIDTH | LENGTH | COMMENTS |
|---|---|---|---|---|---|
| 1 | Top | ¾" | 12" | 18" | |
| 1 | Back apron | ¾" | 5" | 11½" | 1" TBE* |
| 2 | Side aprons | ¾" | 5" | 8¾" | ⅞" TBE* |
| 1 | Front apron | ¾" | 1" | 11" | ¾" TBE* |
| 1 | Front stretcher | ¾" | 1" | 11" | ¾" TBE* |
| 2 | Side stretchers | ¾" | 1" | 8¾" | ⅞" TBE* |
| 1 | Drawer back | ½" | 3" | 9½" | Grooved for drawer bottom |
| 1 | Drawer bottom | ¼" | 7" | 9" | |
| 1 | Drawer front | ¾" | 3" | 9½" | Grooved for drawer bottom |
| 4 | Drawer rails | ¾" | 1" | 8¾" | 1" TBE* |
| 2 | Drawer guides | ¾" | 1¾" | 7½" | |
| 2 | Drawer sides | ½" | 3" | 7½" | Grooved for bottom; length varies with joinery |
| 4 | Legs | ¾" | 2¾" | 27¼" | Front legs have inlaid or inset petals |
| 2 | Stem details | ½" | 5⁄16" | 27¼" | Applied to front legs |

Additional Materials: 1 drawer pull (see Hardware Resources, page 25)

* Tenon both ends

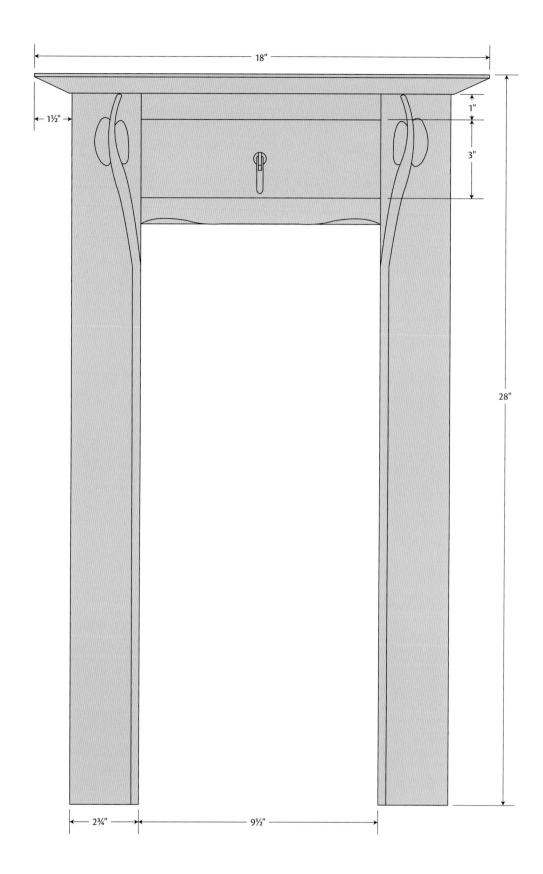

18"

1½"

1"

3"

28"

2¾"

9½"

**ELEVATION**

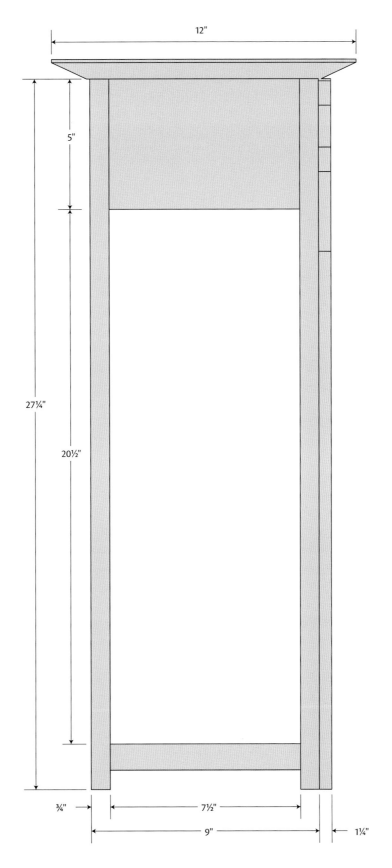

**PROFILE**

TOP

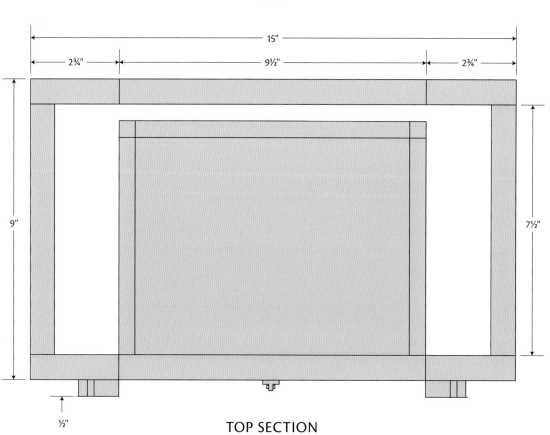

TOP SECTION

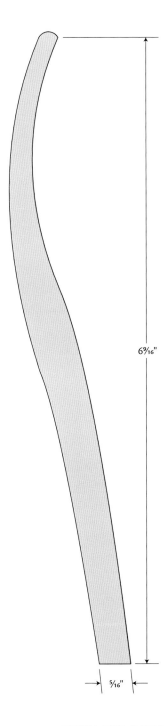

6⁹⁄₁₆"

⁵⁄₁₆"

STEM TIP DETAIL

# DUNGLASS CASTLE BED

83¼" high x 76" wide x 86" deep
(c. 1900)

THOUGH LESS ORNATE than some of Mackintosh's other beds, this design still features organic ornament in the medallions on the sides of the canopy and in the footboard's stylized flower. Four posts anchor the frame and panels used to join headboard and footboard, the latter showing a more complicated four-panel con-struction. The original design has been modified here to accommodate a queen-sized mattress. The same hardware used to join the rails to the ends can also be used to join the canopy rails to the posts. Contemporary photos show it dark, not painted, distinguishing it from other Mackintosh beds.

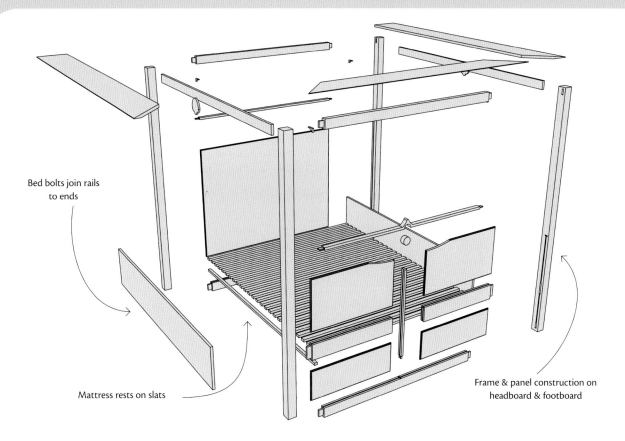

Bed bolts join rails to ends

Mattress rests on slats

Frame & panel construction on headboard & footboard

**EXPLODED VIEW**

# DUNGLASS CASTLE BED

| QUANTITY | DESCRIPTION | THICKNESS | WIDTH | LENGTH | COMMENTS |
|---|---|---|---|---|---|
| **Canopy** | | | | | |
| 1 | Frame end | ¾" | 9¼" | 76" | |
| 2 | Frame sides | ¾" | 9¼" | 86" | |
| 2 | Medallions | ½" | 4⁷⁄₁₆" | 4¾" | |
| 2 | Rails | ¾" | 2¾" | 74½" | Bed bolts join rails to ends |
| 2 | Stretchers | 1½" | 2¾" | 61½" | 1½" TBE* |
| 4 | Corbels | ½" | 1" | 2" | |
| **Headboard** | | | | | |
| 1 | Cap rail | ¾" | 1½" | 61½" | 1½" TBE*; grooved for panel |
| 1 | Panel | ¾" | 44" | 59" | 1¼" tongue all around |
| 1 | Bottom rail | 1½" | 3¼" | 61½" | 1½" TBE*; grooved for panel |
| **Footboard** | | | | | |
| 1 | Medallion | 1½" | 2½" | 2½" | |
| 1 | Cap rail | 1½" | 2¾" | 61½" | 1½" TBE*; grooved for top panels |
| 2 | Top panels | ¾" | 16½" | 29⅜" | ¼ tongue all around |
| 2 | Middle stretchers | 1½" | 5" | 30⅝" | 1½" tenon outside end; ¼" tenon inside end; grooved for panels |
| 2 | Lower panels | ¾" | 10" | 29⅜" | ¼" tongue all around |
| 1 | Center divider | ¾" | 1½" | 30⁵⁄₁₆" | double 1" tenon bottom end; grooved for panels |
| 1 | Bottom rail | 1½" | 3¼" | 61½" | 1½" TBE*; grooved for lower panels; mortised for center divider |
| **Base** | | | | | |
| 2 | Cleats | ¾" | 1" | 74⅜" | |
| 4 | Posts | 2¾" | 2¾" | 82½" | Grooved for panels (see detail on page 46 for footboard posts) |
| 26 | Slats | ¾" | 1½" | 62" | |
| 2 | Side rails | ¾" | 13" | 74½" | Bed bolts join rails to ends |

\* Tenon both ends

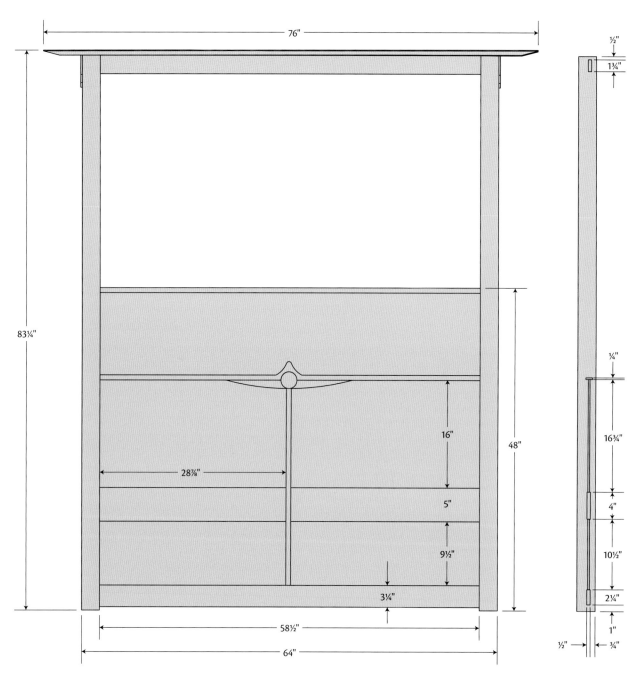

76"

83¼"

48"

16"

5"

9½"

28⅞"

3¼"

58½"

64"

½"

1¾"

¼"

16¾"

4"

10½"

2¼"

1"

½"

¾"

ELEVATION

FOOTBOARD
POST MORTISE
DETAIL

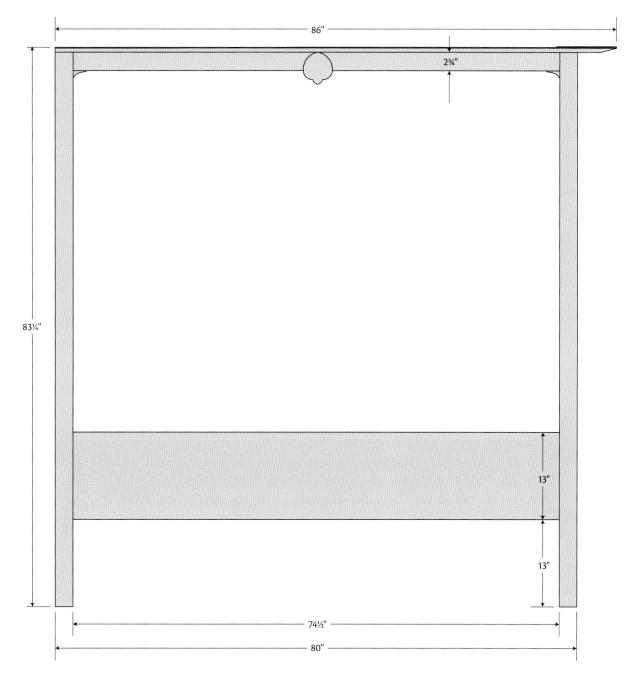

PROFILE

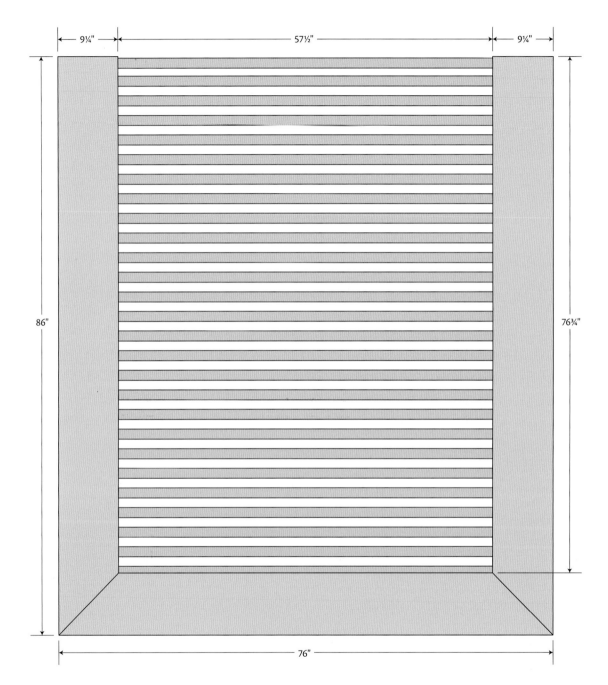

9¼"    57½"    9¼"

86"    76¾"

76"

TOP PLAN

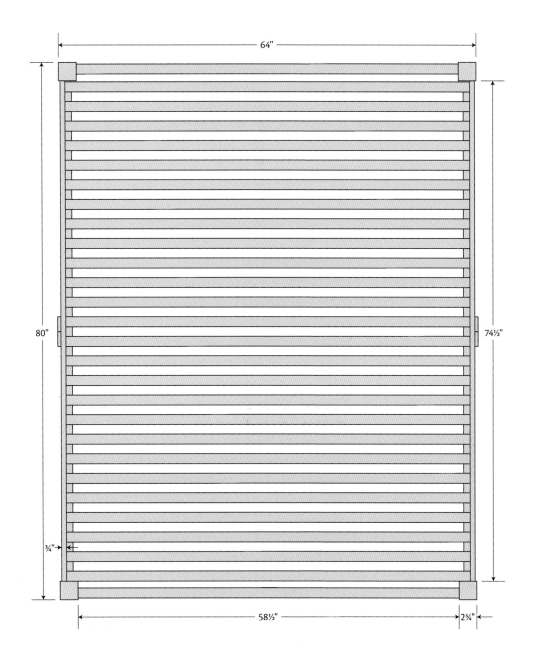

BASE PLAN

# DRESSING TABLE

68" high x 46" wide x 20" deep
(1916)

MACKINTOSH DESIGNED this dressing table for Bassett-Lowke's Derngate residence. It, like much of the furniture made for the client, was assembled in a prisoner-of-war camp on the Isle of Man. Two mahogany cabinets top a low dresser and support a large mirror over an ebonized base. The mirror frame extends the vertical line of the cabinets as well as tying the top and base together. The beveled drawer fronts and inlaid mother-of-pearl squares relieve an otherwise austere façade.

# DRESSING TABLE

| QUANTITY | DESCRIPTION | THICKNESS | WIDTH | LENGTH | COMMENTS |
|---|---|---|---|---|---|
| **Case** | | | | | |
| 2 | Base front/back | ¾" | 2" | 42½" | |
| 4 | Base supports | ¾" | 2" | 16" | Glued & screwed to base front/back |
| 2 | Case sides | ¾" | 20" | 20" | Mitered top/bottom; rabbeted for back |
| 2 | Case top & bottom | ¾" | 20" | 45" | Mitered ends; rabbeted for back |
| 1 | Back | ½" | 19¼" | 44¼" | |
| 1 | Center drawer guide | ¾" | 4" | 14⅞" | Glued to center web frame stile** |
| 3 | Web frame stiles | ¾" | 2" | 14⅞" | Tongued outside edge L/R; ¾" TBE |
| 2 | Web frame rails | 3/4" | 2 | 44" | ⅜" TBE* |
| 1 | Vertical divider | ¾" | 2" | 9" | |
| **Drawers** | | | | | |
| 2 | Large sides | ¾" | 8¼" | 16⅞" | |
| 2 | Large front/back | ¾" | 8¼" | 43½" | |
| 1 | Large applied front | ¾" | 9⅛" | 44¼" | Beveled front edges |
| 2 | Large bottom panels | ¼" | 15⅞" | 20¾" | |
| 1 | Large bottom center rail | ¾" | 1½" | 15⅞" | ¼" TBE*; grooved for drawer bottom panels |
| 4 | Small sides | ¾" | 8½" | 16⅞" | Grooved for drawer bottom |
| 4 | Small front/back | ¾" | 8½" | 21⅜" | |
| 2 | Small applied fronts | ¾" | 9⅜" | 22⅛" | Beveled front edges |
| 2 | Small bottoms | ¼" | 16⅛" | 20⅜" | |
| **Mirror** | | | | | |
| 1 | Large bottom rail | ¾" | 3¼" | 22⅞" | Mitered ends; cut front concave shape |
| 2 | Long stiles | 1" | 1½" | 65¾" | Mitered top; notched to meet case sides |
| 1 | Mirror | ⅛" | 22¾" | 44⅞" | |
| 1 | Backing board | ¼" | 22¾" | 44⅞" | |
| 2 | Short stiles | 1" | 1½" | 45⁷⁄₁₆" | Mitered top |
| 1 | Top rail | 1" | 1½" | 46" | Mitered both ends |
| **Upper Cabinets** | | | | | |
| 4 | Sides | ½" | 9" | 26" | Mitered top edge; rabbeted for back & bottom |
| 8 | Shelves | ½" | 7⅞" | 10" | Installed with adjustable shelf hardware |
| 2 | Backs | ½" | 10½" | 25½" | |
| 2 | Bottoms | ½" | 8¾" | 10½" | Rabbeted for back |
| 2 | Lower rails | ½" | 2¼" | 11" | ½" TBE* |
| 2 | Tops | ½" | 9" | 11" | Mitered both ends |
| 4 | Door long mouldings | ⅛" | ⅝" | 23" | Mitered both ends |
| 2 | Door panels | ½" | 9" | 22" | ¼" tongue all around |
| 4 | Door rails | ½" | 1" | 8¾" | ½" TBE*; grooved for door panels |
| 4 | Door stiles | ½" | 1" | 22¾" | Grooved for door panels |
| 4 | Door short mouldings | ⅛" | ⅝" | 10" | Mitered both ends |

\* Tenon both ends

\*\* Web frame glued & screwed together

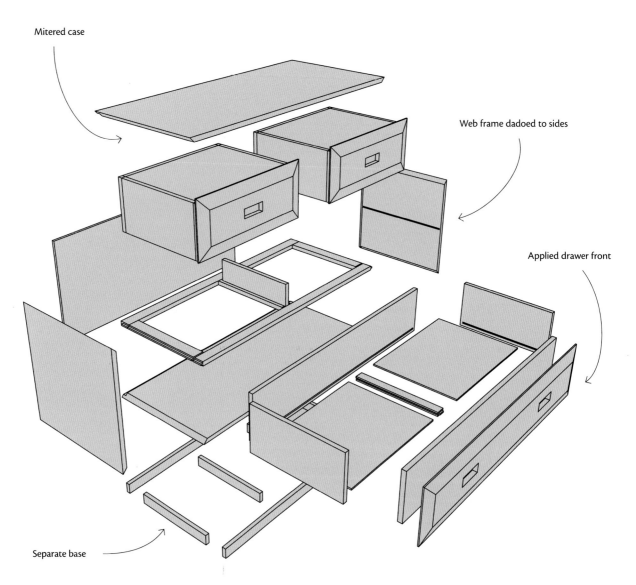

Mitered case

Web frame dadoed to sides

Applied drawer front

Separate base

**BOTTOM CASE, EXPLODED VIEW**

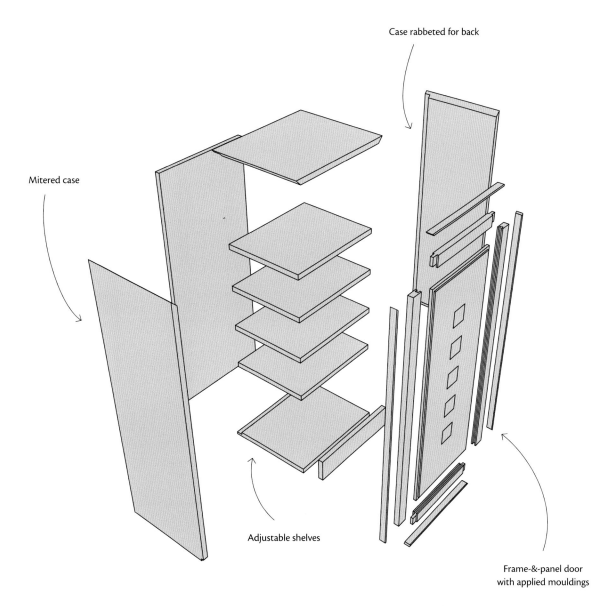

Case rabbeted for back

Mitered case

Adjustable shelves

Frame-&-panel door
with applied mouldings

**UPPER CABINET, EXPLODED VIEW**

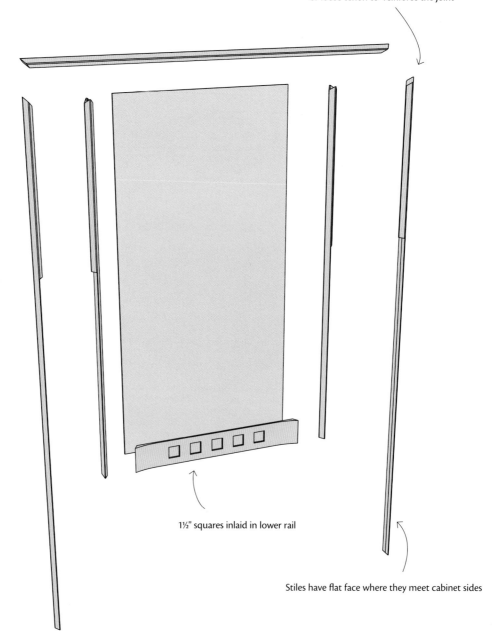

Frame mitered together; use a spline, biscuit
or loose tenon to reinforce the joint

1½" squares inlaid in lower rail

Stiles have flat face where they meet cabinet sides

## MIRROR, EXPLODED VIEW

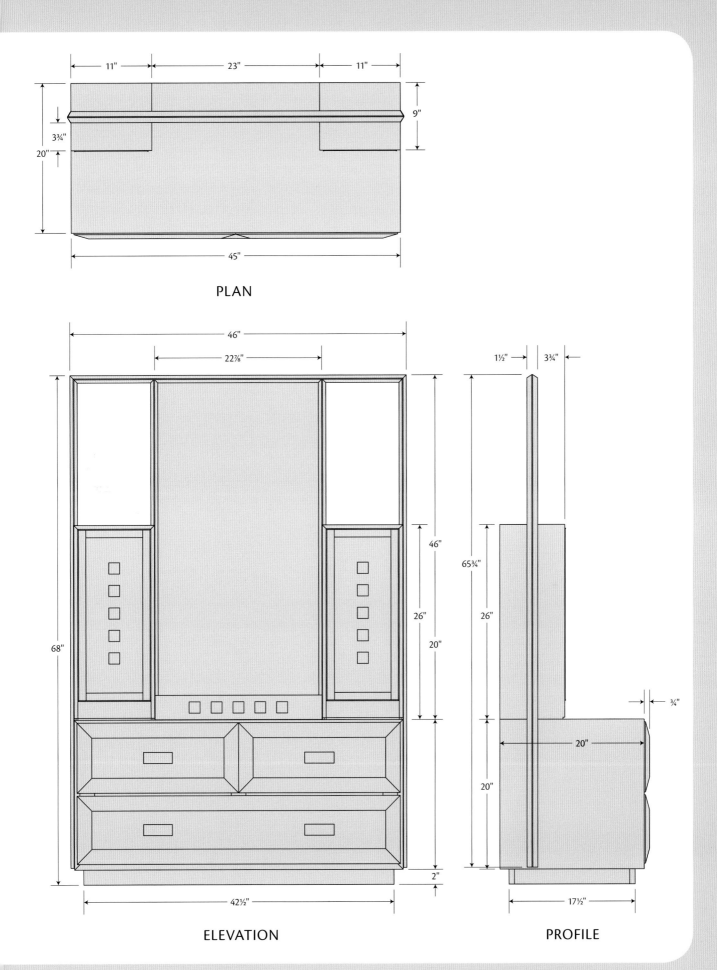

PLAN

ELEVATION

PROFILE

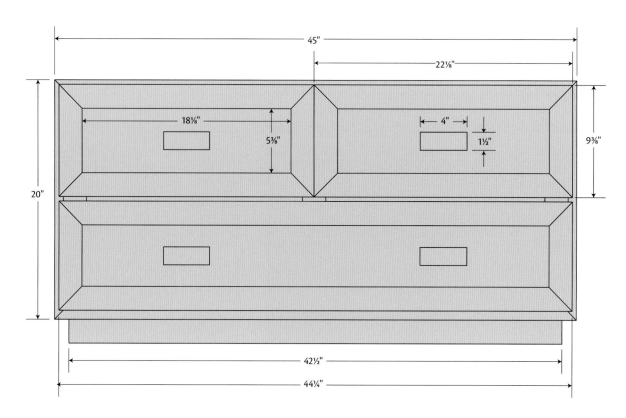

BASE ELEVATION

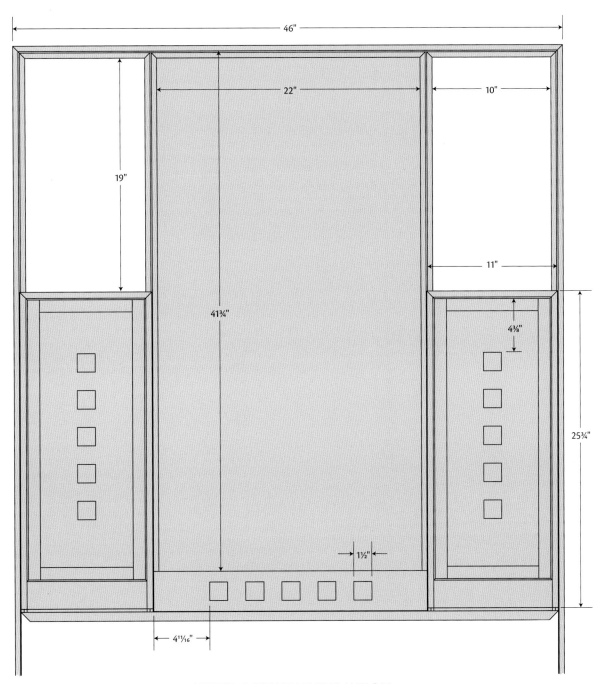

UPPER ASSEMBLY ELEVATION

# TOWEL RAIL

28" high x 24" wide x 7¼" deep
(1916), mahogany

LAP JOINTS FEATURE heavily in this towel rail, forming the grid in sides and bottom, while mortises and tenons join the sides to the body. The simple construction techniques belie the appeal of the piece; it sold at auction in 2002 for $29,751. It would also make an attractive quilt stand. If building for that use, consider adding some additional width to the design.

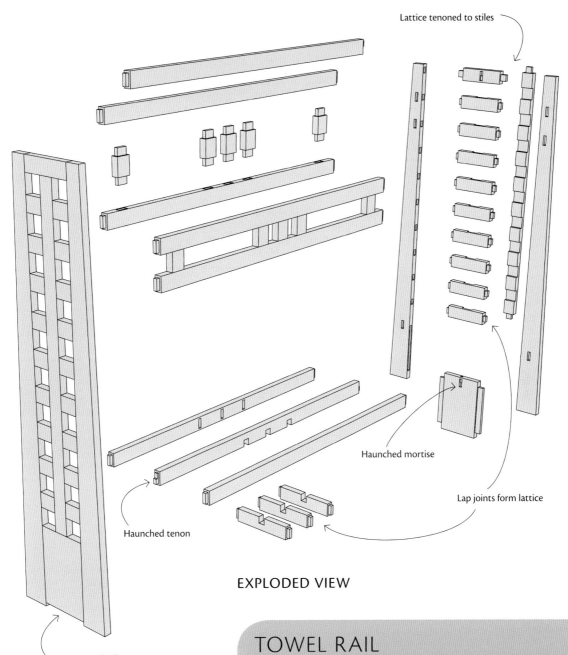

Lattice tenoned to stiles

Haunched mortise

Lap joints form lattice

Haunched tenon

Lower rail offset so stiles form feet

**EXPLODED VIEW**

## TOWEL RAIL

| QUANTITY | DESCRIPTION | THICKNESS | WIDTH | LENGTH | COMMENTS |
|---|---|---|---|---|---|
| 1 | Top | ½" | 1" | 23½" | ¼" TBE* |
| **Middle** | | | | | |
| 4 | Rails | ½" | 1" | 23½" | ¼" TBE* |
| 10 | Stiles | ½" | 1" | 2¼" | ½" TBE* |
| **Sides** | | | | | |
| 2 | Bottom rails | ½" | 5¼" | 4½" | ½" TBE* |
| 18 | Center rails | ½" | 1" | 4" | ¼" TBE* |
| 2 | Center stiles | ½" | 1" | 22½" | ½" TBE* |
| 4 | Outer stiles | ½" | 1⅞" | 28" | |
| 2 | Top rails | ½" | 1" | 4½" | ½" TBE* |
| **Bottom** | | | | | |
| 2 | Outer rails | ½" | 1" | 23½" | ¼" TBE* |
| 1 | Center rail | ½" | 1" | 23½" | ¼" TBE* |
| 3 | Crosspieces | ½" | 1" | 5" | ¼" TBE* |

* Tenon both ends

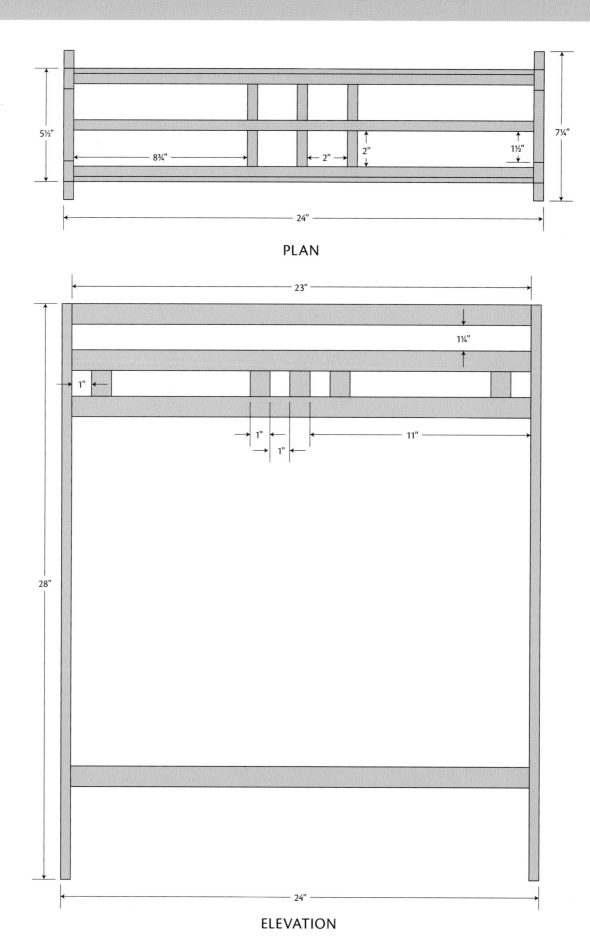

PLAN

ELEVATION

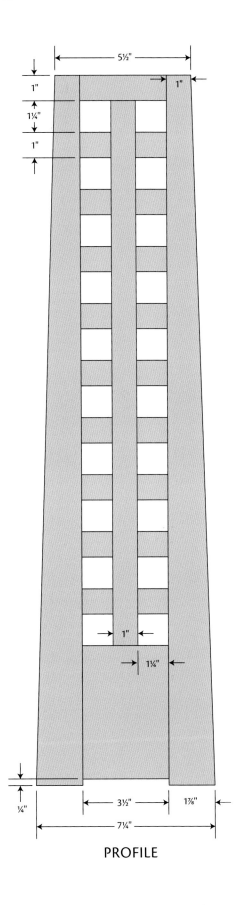

PROFILE

# HOUS'HILL WASHSTAND

63¼" high x 51¼" wide x 20⅜" deep
(1904), stained oak
and leaded glass

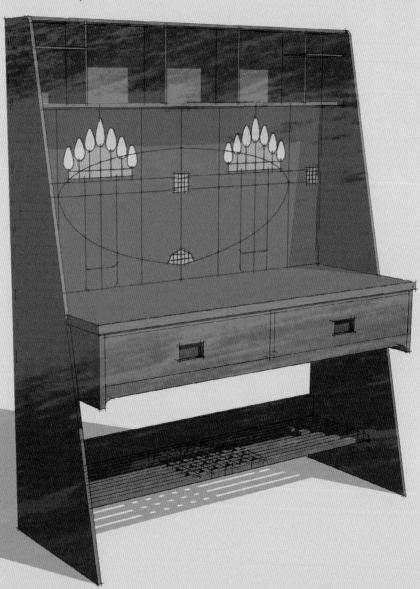

**D**ESIGNED FOR THE Blue Bedroom in Hous'hill, this washstand is an interesting study in contrasts. It pairs sharp angles and straight lines with an elaborate organiform leaded glass backsplash and vibrant ceramic tile counter. The tapered sides capture an upper shelf, floating drawers and gridwork lower shelf. Francis Smith was paid £6 ($767) for the case, McCullock £3.50 ($447) for the glass.

Although the modern home doesn't often call for a washstand, the piece would also make an attractive serving table, bar or even cabinet for a sink. With slight modification, the base could also include additional drawers or cupboards, expanding storage.

## HOUS'HILL WASHSTAND

| QUANTITY | DESCRIPTION | THICKNESS | WIDTH | LENGTH | COMMENTS |
|---|---|---|---|---|---|
| 1 | Back panel | ½" | 23" | 50¼" | |
| 2 | Sides | ½" | 20⅜" | 63¼" | ⅛" TBE* |
| 1 | Counter back | ¾" | 8¾" | 50¾" | ¼" double TBE* |
| 1 | Center divider | ¾" | ¾" | 6½" | ½" TBE* |
| 1 | Lower rail | ¾" | 2" | 49¾" | ½" double TBE* |
| 1 | Top stretcher | ¾" | 1" | 49½" | ⅜" dovetail both ends |
| 1 | Center drawer divider | ¾" | 2" | 18⅞" | |
| 1 | Center drawer runner | ¾" | 2¾" | 19⅜" | ¼" TBE* |
| 2 | Counter sides | ¾" | 8¾" | 20" | Tenoned to case back |
| 2 | Counter side trim pieces | ¼" | 1" | 7 1⁄16" | Angle cut one end to meet sides |
| 1 | Countertop | ¾" | 19⅝" | 50¼" | |
| 2 | Cleats | ¾" | 1" | 18⅝" | Butt joined using glue and/or screws |
| 2 | Side drawer runners | ¾" | 1" | 18⅞" | |
| 1 | Front counter trim | ¼" | 1" | 50¾" | Mitered both ends |
| 1 | Long shelf | ½" | 4¾" | 50¾" | ¼" TBE* |
| 2 | Small shelves | ¼" | 4¾" | 7⅝" | ⅛" TBE* |
| 1 | Top | ⅜" | 5½" | 50¾" | ¼" TBE*; rabbeted for back panel |
| 4 | Vertical dividers | ¼" | 4¾" | 9⅝" | ⅛" TBE* |
| 2 | Side glass cleats | ¼" | ¼" | 22¾" | |
| 1 | Top glass cleat | ¼" | ¼" | 50¼" | |
| Bottom Shelf | | | | | |
| 1 | Stretcher | ¾" | 4" | 50¾" | ¼" TBE* |
| 6 | Long slats | ¾" | 1" | 50¾" | ¼" TBE* |
| 6 | Short slats | ¾" | 1" | 11¼" | ½" TBE* |
| Drawers | | | | | |
| 2 | Backs | ½" | 5½" | 24" | Grooved for drawer bottom |
| 2 | Bottoms | ¼" | 18" | 23½" | |
| 2 | Fronts | ¾" | 5½" | 24" | Grooved for drawer bottom |
| 4 | Sides | ½" | 5½" | 18½" | Grooved for drawer bottom |

* Tenon both ends

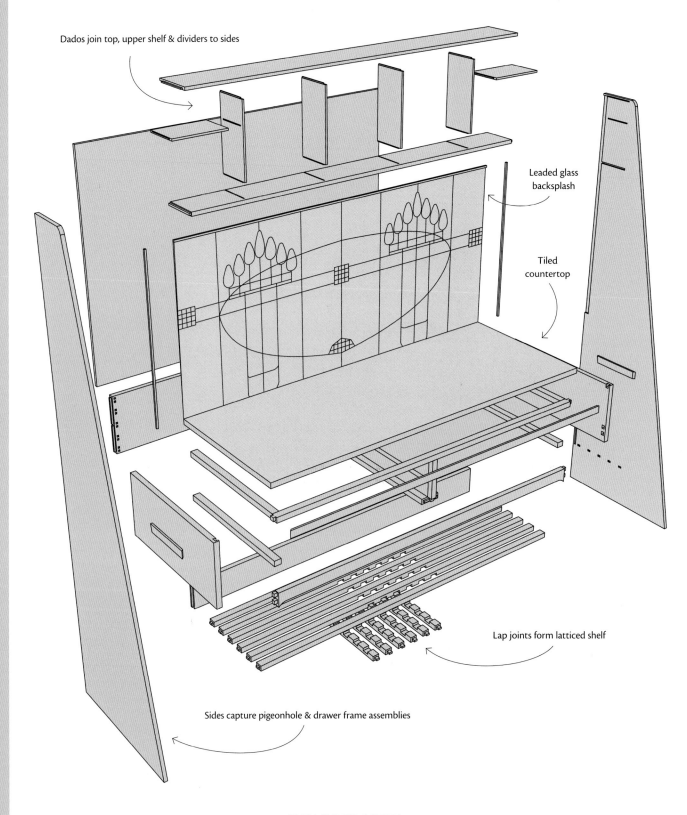

Dados join top, upper shelf & dividers to sides

Leaded glass backsplash

Tiled countertop

Lap joints form latticed shelf

Sides capture pigeonhole & drawer frame assemblies

**EXPLODED VIEW**

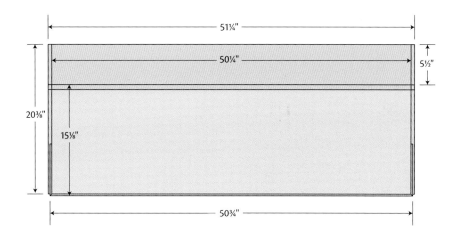

PLAN

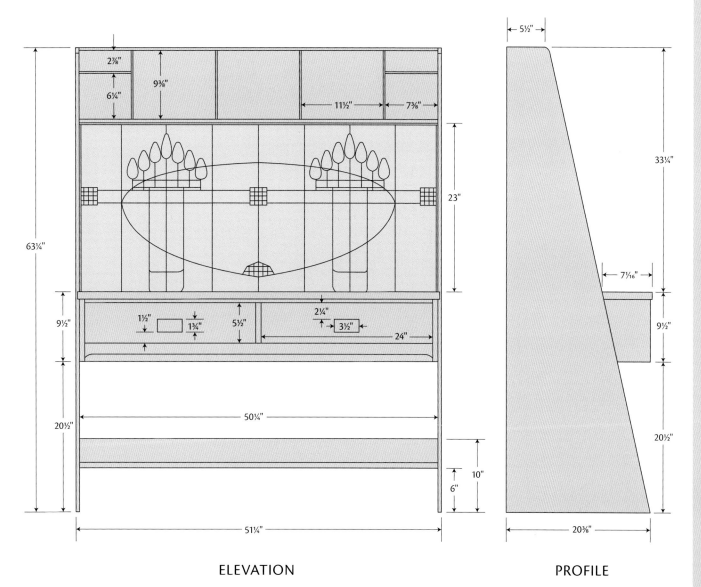

ELEVATION

PROFILE

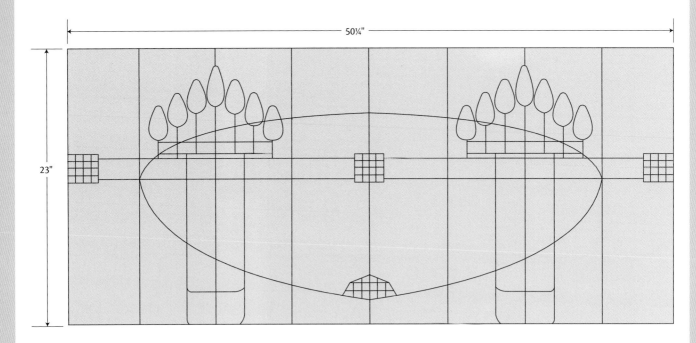

GLASS PANEL DETAIL

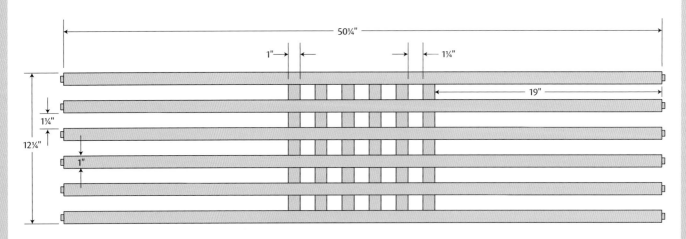

LATTICE SHELF DETAIL PLAN

# CHIMNEY CUPBOARD

66" high x 15" wide x 13" deep
(1904), stained oak

LIKE THE WASHSTAND (page 62), this chimney cupboard was designed for the Blue Bedroom at Hous'hill. One stands on either side of a canopy bed (a similar design for the main bedroom at Hill House integrates the cabinets into the headboard). A stained glass panel can be added to the alcove between the top and lower cabinet (omitted from the drawings here). This optional feature would catch the light of a lamp or candle to striking effect.

The wide bottom rail and position of the lower cabinet's bottom shelf creates a fair amount of dead space in the design. With little modification, this space could be transformed into a secret compartment.

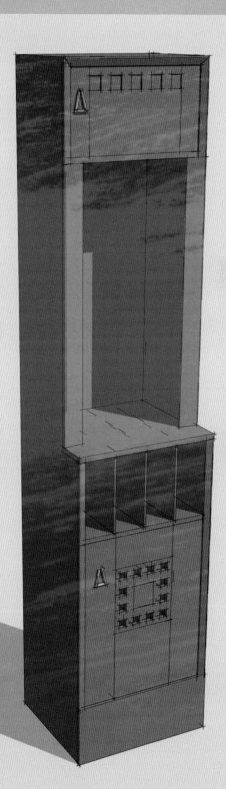

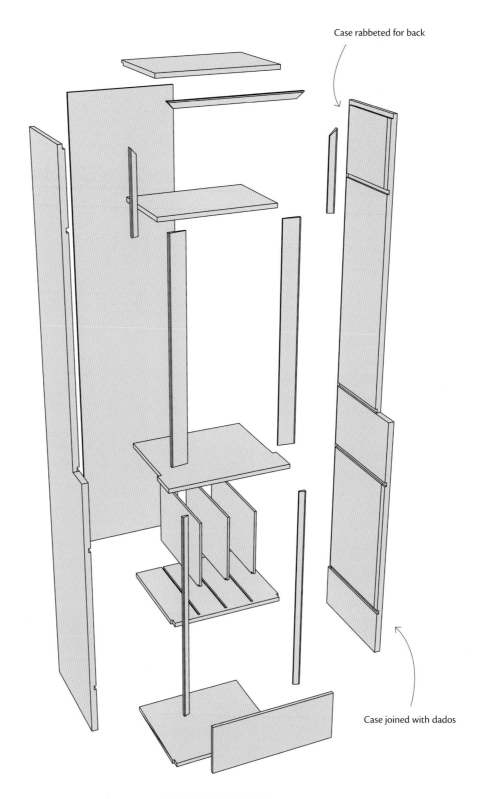

Case rabbeted for back

Case joined with dados

**EXPLODED VIEW**

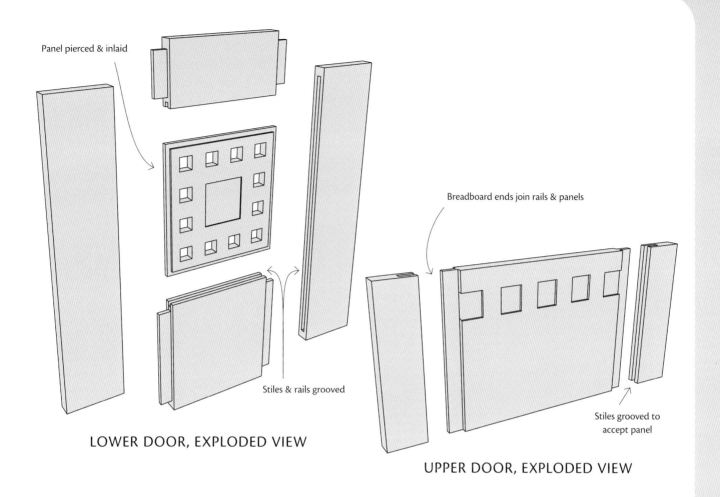

Panel pierced & inlaid

Breadboard ends join rails & panels

Stiles & rails grooved

Stiles grooved to accept panel

**LOWER DOOR, EXPLODED VIEW**

**UPPER DOOR, EXPLODED VIEW**

# CHIMNEY CUPBOARD

| QUANTITY | DESCRIPTION | THICKNESS | WIDTH | LENGTH | COMMENTS |
|---|---|---|---|---|---|
| 1 | Back | ¼" | 14" | 60 ¼" | |
| 2 | Sides | ¾" | 12⅝" | 66" | |
| 1 | Top | ½" | 9⅝" | 14" | Rabbeted for back |
| 1 | Shallow shelf | ½" | 9⅛" | 14" | |
| 2 | Top section trim stiles | ⅜" | ¾" | 8¾" | Mitered |
| 1 | Top trim rail | ⅜" | ¾" | 15" | Mitered |
| 2 | Center section trim stiles | ⅜" | 2" | 25 ½" | Tapered across width |
| 1 | Counter | ½" | 12½" | 15" | |
| 1 | Deep shelf | ½" | 12⅛" | 14" | Dadoed for vertical dividers |
| 3 | Vertical dividers | ¼" | 8¼" | 12⅛" | |
| 2 | Lower section trim stiles | ⅜" | ¾" | 25¼" | |
| 1 | Bottom | ½" | 12⅛" | 14" | |
| 1 | Bottom rail | ¾" | 6" | 15" | Nailed or screwed in place |
| 1 | Lower door bottom rail | ¾" | 7" | 8" | ¾" TBE* |
| 1 | Lower door panel | ½" | 7" | 7¼" | ¼" tongue all around |
| 2 | Lower door stiles | ¾" | 3½" | 17" | Grooved for door panel & rails |
| 1 | Lower door upper rail | ¾" | 3¼" | 8" | ¾" TBE* |
| 2 | Upper door breadboard ends | ¾" | 2" | 7¾" | Grooved for door panel |
| 1 | Upper door panel | ¾" | 7¾" | 11" | ¾" TBE* |

Additional Materials: 2 pulls (see Hardware Resources, page 25)

* Tenon both ends

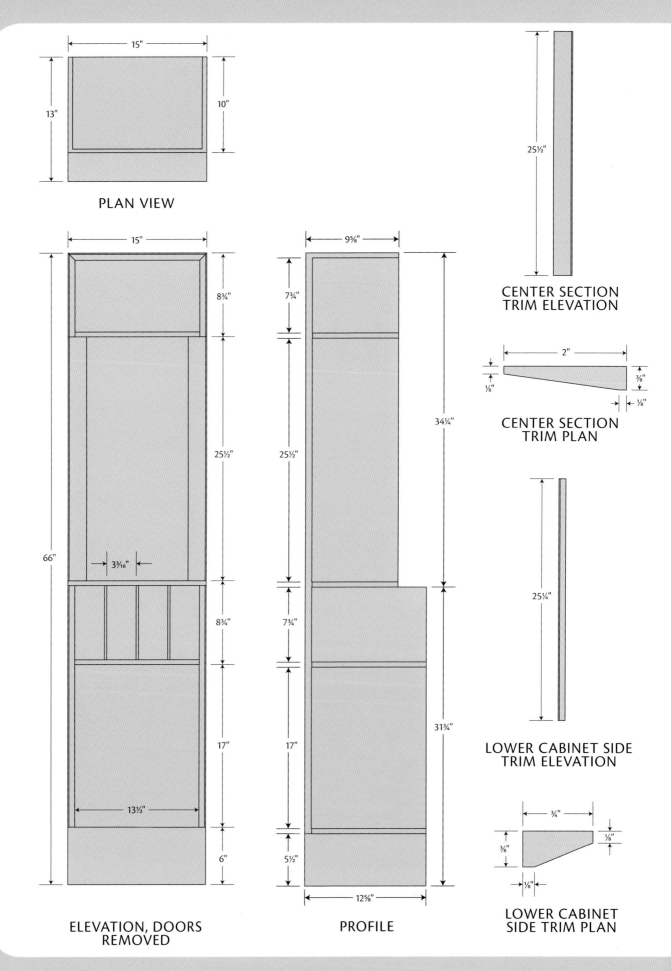

PLAN VIEW

15"
13"
10"

CENTER SECTION
TRIM ELEVATION

25½"

CENTER SECTION
TRIM PLAN

2"
3/8"
1/8"
1/8"

15"
8¾"
25½"
66"
3 3/16"
8¾"
17"
13½"
6"

ELEVATION, DOORS
REMOVED

9⅝"
7¾"
25½"
34¼"
7¾"
17"
31¾"
5½"
12⅝"

PROFILE

LOWER CABINET SIDE
TRIM ELEVATION

25¼"

LOWER CABINET
SIDE TRIM PLAN

¾"
1/8"
3/8"
1/8"

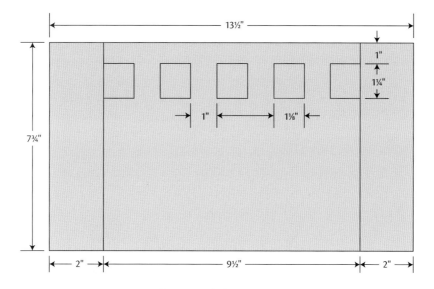

UPPER DOOR ELEVATION

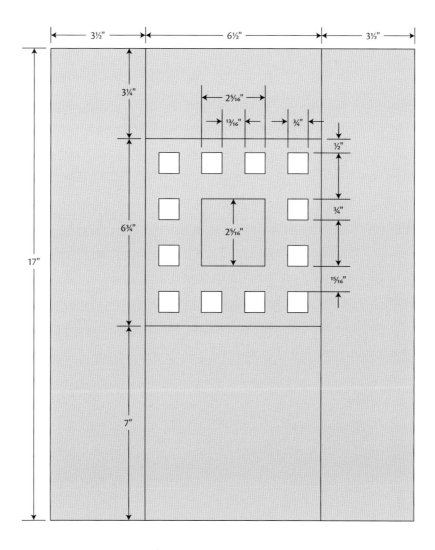

LOWER DOOR ELEVATION

# MAINS STREET DINING TABLE

30" high x 78" wide x 33" deep
(1900), oak, stained dark

A LARGE OVERHANG and arched aprons pierced by organic cutouts with applied carvings lighten what might have been an otherwise massive design in this table Mackintosh created for his own home. The battened top is supported by a simple base. The rectangular form is easily modified to adapt the design to different spaces. Mackintosh also designed a smaller, square table to act as an extension – a novel solution for occasions requiring more seating. Although there's no record of the extension being built, Mackintosh took a similar approach when designing the hall table and extension for Windyhill.

As drawn, the table features detachable legs to allow for easy transport. If transportation isn't a concern, mortises and tenons can be used to join the legs to the stretchers, requiring additional material in the length of the stretchers to form the tenons.

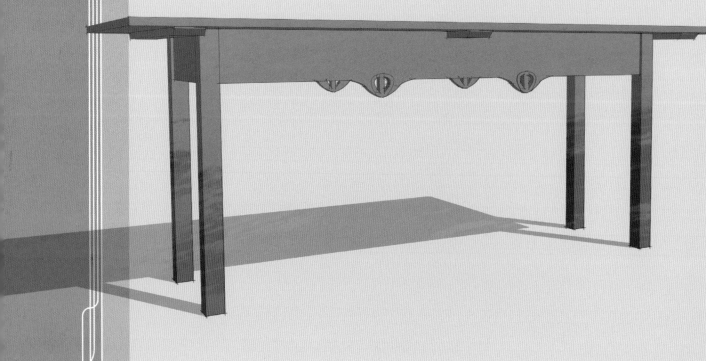

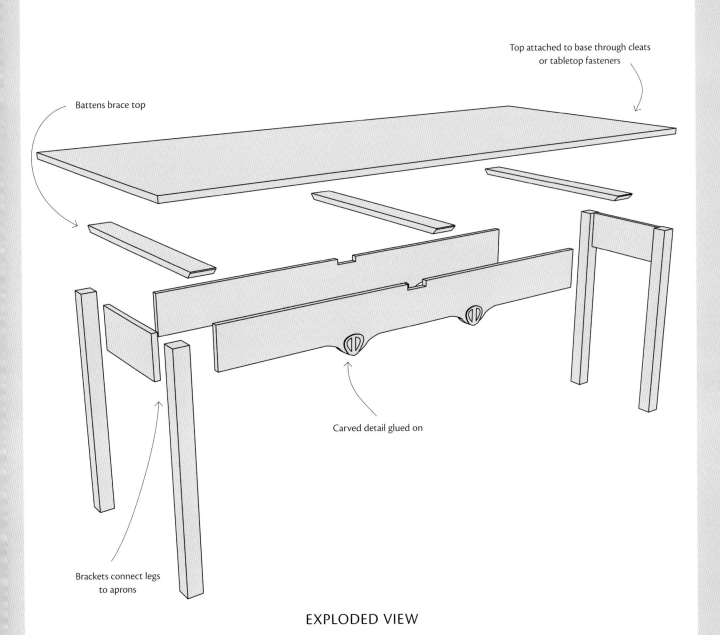

Battens brace top

Top attached to base through cleats
or tabletop fasteners

Carved detail glued on

Brackets connect legs
to aprons

EXPLODED VIEW

# MAINS STREET DINING TABLE

| QUANTITY | DESCRIPTION | THICKNESS | WIDTH | LENGTH | COMMENTS |
|---|---|---|---|---|---|
| 4 | Legs | 2" | 2" | 29¼" | Brackets join legs to aprons |
| 2 | Long aprons | ¾" | 7½" | 58" | Carved detail applied to piercing |
| 2 | Short aprons | ¾" | 5½" | 13" | |
| 1 | Top | ¾" | 33" | 78" | |
| 3 | Battens | ¾" | 3" | 27" | |
| 4 | Applied carvings | ⅛" | 2¹⁵⁄₁₆" | 2¹¹⁄₁₆" | |

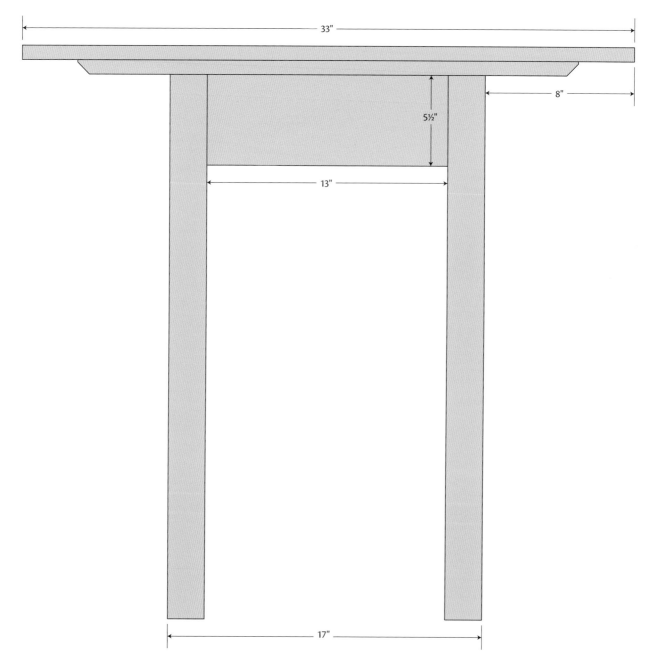

33"

8"

5½"

13"

17"

PROFILE

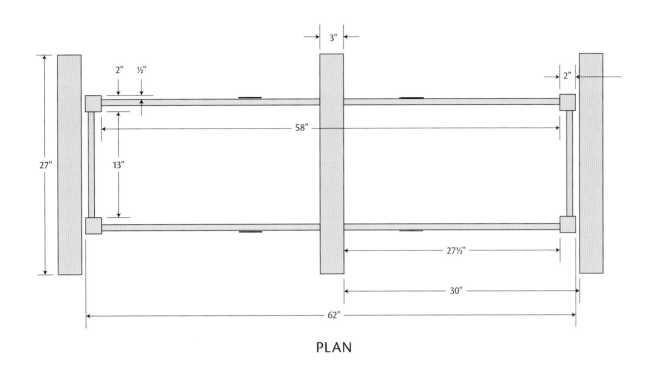

PLAN

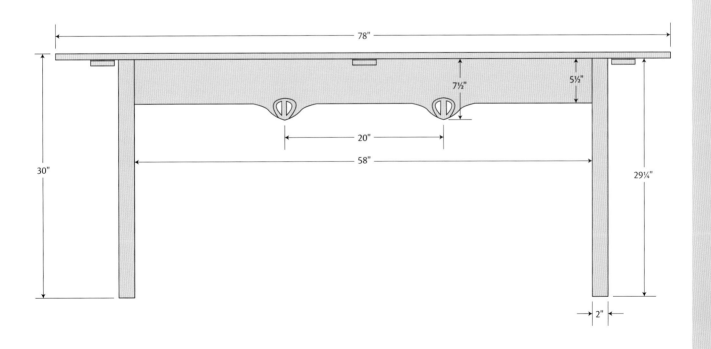

ELEVATION

# HIGH BACK CHAIR

60" high x 19" wide x 18" deep
(1900)

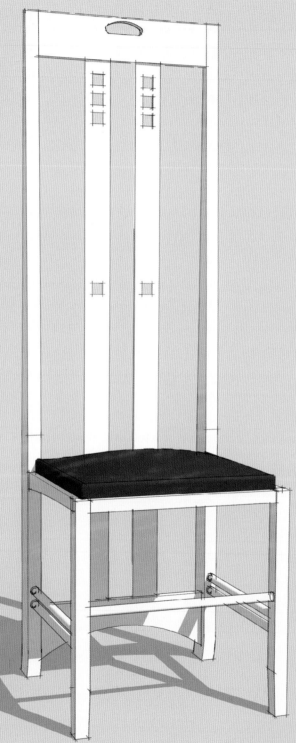

THE HIGH BACK GIVES this chair a stately grace and helps to isolate a group seated around a table, but it doesn't necessarily make for comfort. Examples built for the Ingram Street Tea Room were stained dark; those in Mackintosh's own home were painted white.

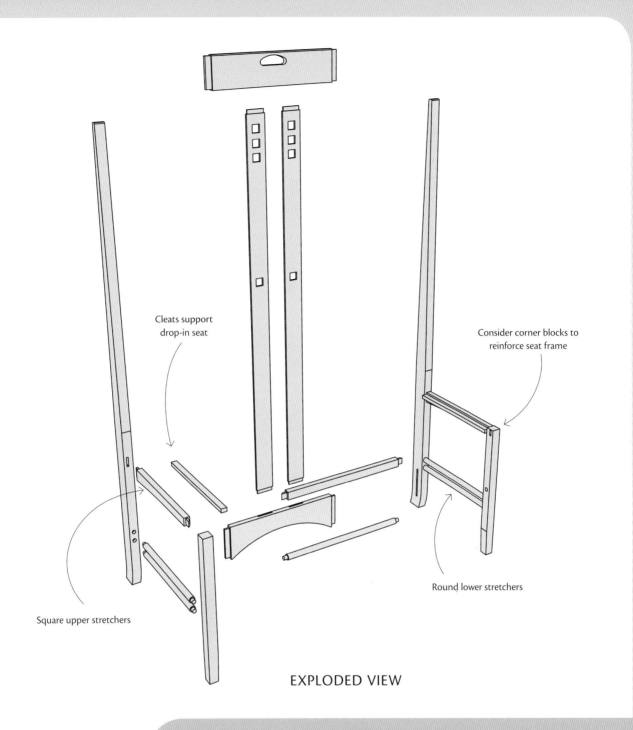

Cleats support
drop-in seat

Consider corner blocks to
reinforce seat frame

Round lower stretchers

Square upper stretchers

**EXPLODED VIEW**

# HIGH BACK CHAIR

| QUANTITY | DESCRIPTION | THICKNESS | WIDTH | LENGTH | COMMENTS |
|---|---|---|---|---|---|
| 2 | Back legs | 1¼" | 2¹¹⁄₁₆" | 60³⁄₁₆" | |
| 2 | Back slats | ¼" | 2½" | 50¾" | ½" TBE* |
| 1 | Back top rail | ¾" | 3¹⁵⁄₁₆" | 18" | ¾" TBE* |
| 1 | Bottom rear stretcher | ¾" | 5" | 18" | ¾" TBE* |
| 1 | Front bottom stretcher | ¾" | ¾" | 17½" | ½" TBE* |
| 2 | Front legs | 1¼" | 1¼" | 19" | |
| 2 | Seat cleats | ½" | ¾" | 14⅛" | |
| 4 | Side stretchers | ¾" | ¾" | 15⅛" | ½" TBE* |
| 1 | Top front stretcher | ¾" | 1" | 18" | ¾" mitered TBE* |
| 2 | Top side stretchers | ¾" | 1½" | 15⅝" | ¾" TBE* (miter front tenon) |

* Tenon both ends

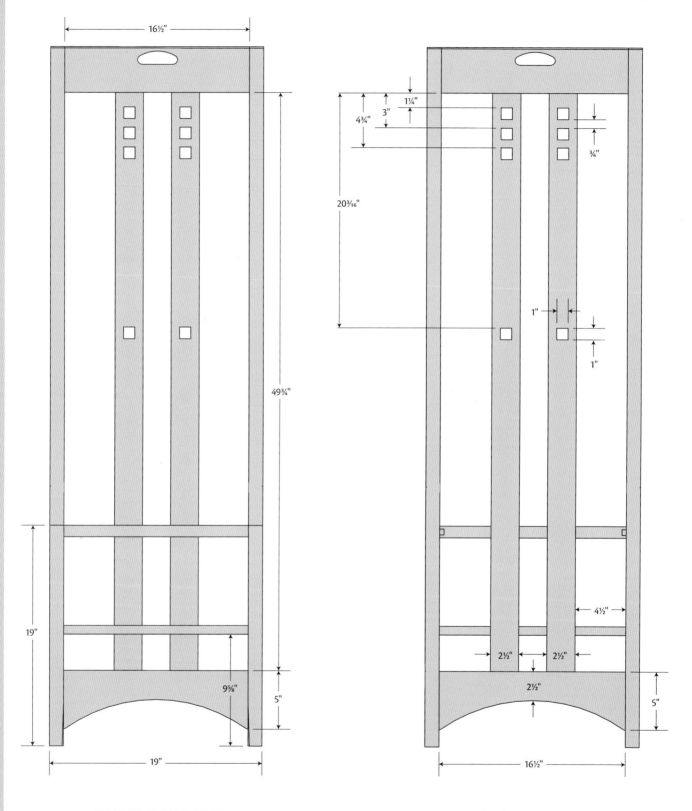

FRONT ELEVATION

BACK ELEVATION

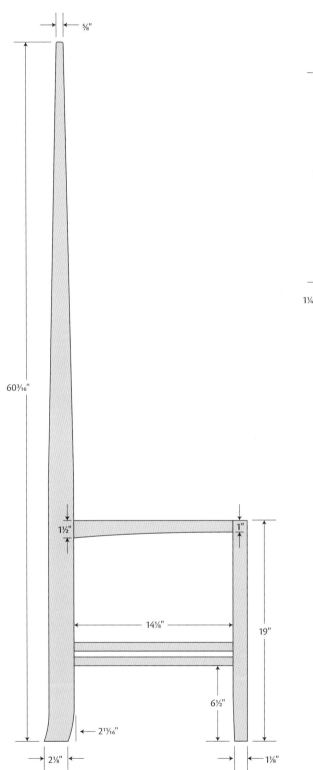

⅝"

60³⁄₁₆"

1½"

1"

14⅛"

19"

6½"

2¹¹⁄₁₆"

2⅛"

1⅛"

**PROFILE**

19"

18"

14⅛"

1¼"

16½"

1¼"

**PLAN**

# SOUTHPARK AVENUE DRESSER

83" high x 83" x 23" deep
(1906), pine, oil cloth

MACKINTOSH DESIGNED this dresser for his home at 78 Southpark Avenue. Though modestly executed in black-stained pine, it still shows care in its design, with the motif of the square on the upper shelves echoed in its overall shape. It is a large piece as designed, but the simplicity of construction and rectilinear form make it easy to scale down. The distinctive and flexible design makes it an interesting alternative to built-in cabinets in the kitchen.

# SOUTHPARK AVENUE DRESSER

| QUANTITY | DESCRIPTION | THICKNESS | WIDTH | LENGTH | COMMENTS |
|---|---|---|---|---|---|
| **Base** | | | | | |
| 2 | Back legs | ¾" | 3" | 18½" | |
| 2 | Front legs | 2" | 3" | 18½" | |
| 2 | Top stretchers | ¾" | 3" | 20" | ⅝" double dovetails both ends |
| 2 | Long stretchers | ¾" | 2" | 80¼" | ½" double TBE* |
| 3 | Bottom stretcher cross pieces | ¾" | 2" | 6½" | ½" double TBE* |
| 2 | Side rails | ¾" | 2" | 19¾" | ½" TBE* |
| **Case** | | | | | |
| 1 | Case back | ½" | 12¼" | 82¼" | |
| 3 | Dividers | ¾" | 12" | 20¾" | ¼" TBE* |
| 2 | Case sides | ¾" | 13" | 21½" | |
| 4 | Web frame rails | ¾" | 1½" | 20⁵⁄₁₆" | ¼" TBE* |
| 4 | Web frame stiles | ¾" | 1¾" | 18¼" | ½" TBE*; ¼" tenon inside edge |
| 2 | Top/bottom | ¾" | 21½" | 81½" | Rabbeted for back |
| 1 | Counter top | 1¼" | 23" | 86" | |
| **Drawers** | | | | | |
| 2 | Large drawer backs | ½" | 11½" | 19⅝" | Grooved for drawer bottom |
| 2 | Large drawer fronts | ¾" | 11½" | 19¹³⁄₁₆" | Grooved for drawer bottom |
| 4 | Large drawer sides | ½" | 11½" | 20" | Grooved for drawer bottom |
| 4 | Small drawer backs | ½" | 5⅜" | 20" | Grooved for drawer bottom |
| 4 | Small drawer fronts | ¾" | 5⅜" | 20" | Grooved for drawer bottom |
| 8 | Small drawer sides | ½" | 5⅜" | 20" | Grooved for drawer bottom |
| 6 | Drawer bottoms | ¼" | 19⅛" | 19¾" | |
| **Hutch** | | | | | |
| 1 | Grid bottom rail | ½" | 3" | 81½" | |
| 7 | Grid rails | ½" | 1½" | 81½" | |
| 15 | Grid stiles | ½" | 1½" | 49½" | |
| 2 | Middle horizontal shelf supports | ⅝" | ¾" | 5½" | ½" TBE* |
| 2 | Middle vertical shelf supports | 1½" | 1½" | 19¹⁵⁄₁₆" | ⅜" TBE* |
| 2 | Shelf sides | ¾" | 7½" | 49⅞" | Dadoed for shelves |
| 1 | Shelf top | ¾" | 7½" | 83" | Rabbeted for sides |
| 2 | Shelf top horizontal supports | ⅝" | ¾" | 5½" | ½" TBE* |
| 2 | Shelf top vertical supports | 1½" | 1½" | 14³⁄₁₆" | ⅜" TBE* |
| 1 | Upper shelf | ¾" | 6½" | 82" | |
| 2 | Upper horizontal shelf supports | ⅝" | ¾" | 5½" | ½" TBE* |
| 2 | Upper vertical shelf supports | 1½" | 1½" | 19¹⁵⁄₁₆" | ⅜" TBE* |
| 1 | Lower shelf | ¾" | 6¾" | 82" | |
| 2 | Lower shelf horizontal supports | ⅝" | ¾" | 5½" | ½" TBE* |
| 2 | Lower shelf vertical supports | 1½" | 1½" | 15¹³⁄₁₆" | ⅜" tenon top end |

Additional materials: 6 drawer pulls (see Hardware Resources, page 25)

* Tenon both ends

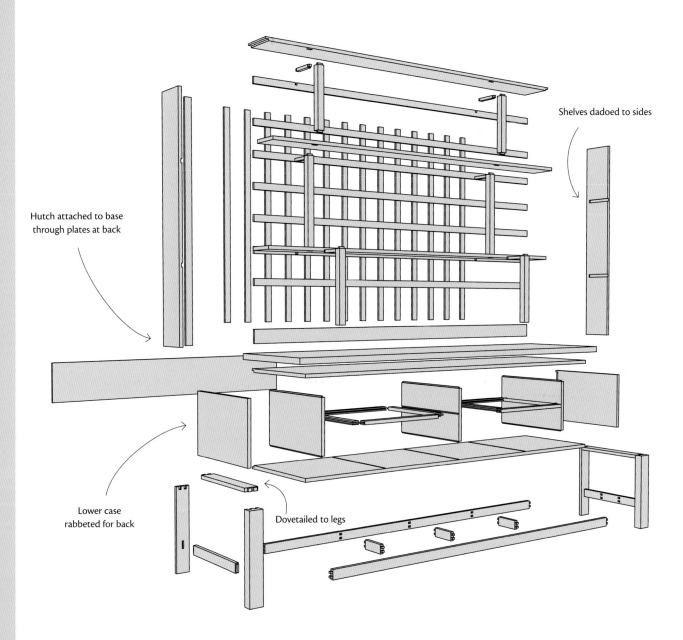

Shelves dadoed to sides

Hutch attached to base through plates at back

Lower case rabbeted for back

Dovetailed to legs

**EXPLODED VIEW**

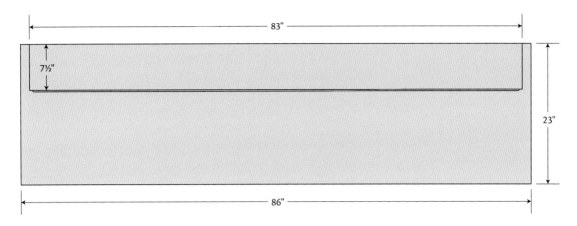

PLAN

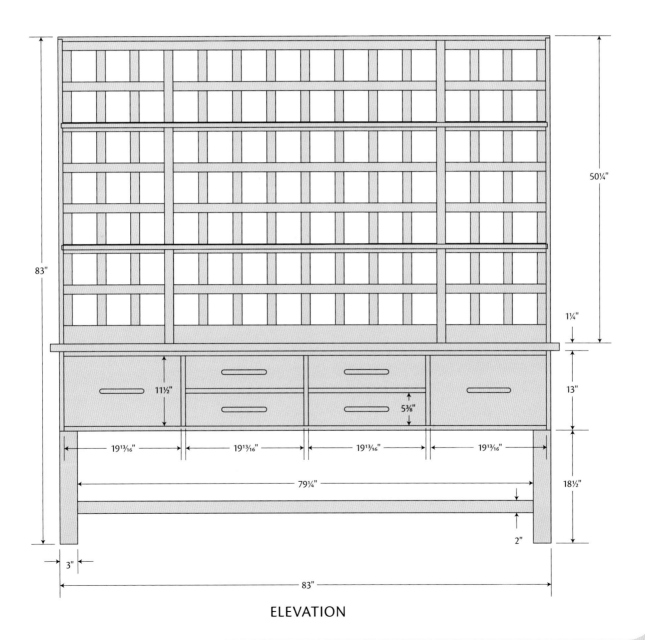

ELEVATION

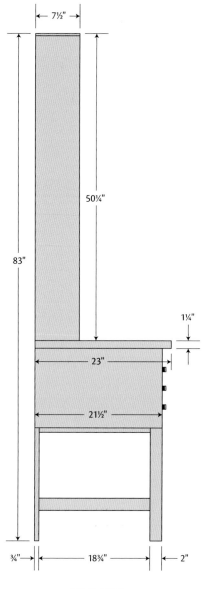

PROFILE

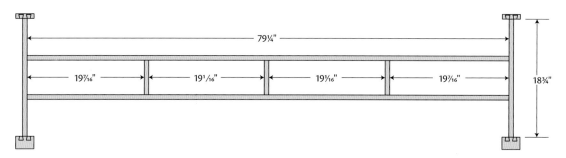

BASE PLAN, RAILS REMOVED

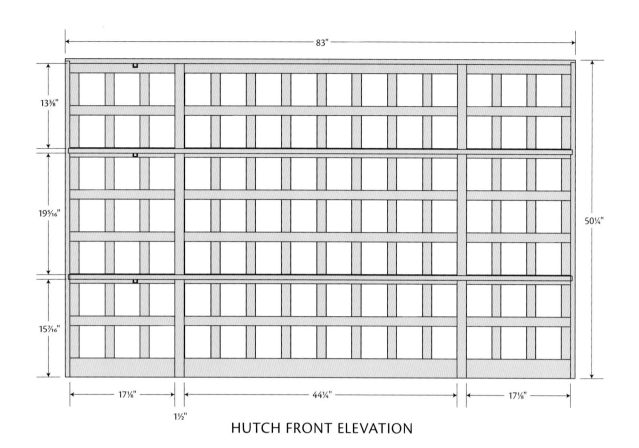

HUTCH FRONT ELEVATION

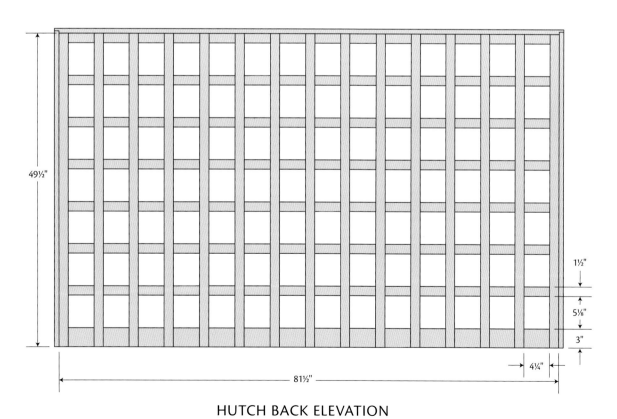

HUTCH BACK ELEVATION

# MAINS STREET SERVING TABLE

30" high x 39" wide x 20" deep
(1900), oak, stained dark

WITH ITS OVERHANGING top, rectilinear form and vertical cutouts, this simple serving table designed for the Mains Street dining room might be Mackintosh's most Mission-like design, an effect heightened by the dark stained oak.

Mortises and tenons join the sides to the apron with the top screwed to the base through table hardware or wooden cleats. The attractive design, small number of parts and simple construction make it a good project for the beginning woodworker.

Top attached to base through cleats
or tabletop fasteners

Rabbets on shelf & stretchers

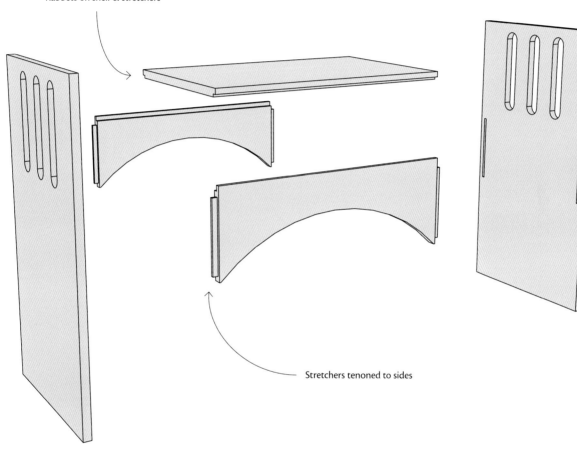

Stretchers tenoned to sides

**EXPLODED VIEW**

# MAINS STREET SERVING TABLE

| QUANTITY | DESCRIPTION | THICKNESS | WIDTH | LENGTH | COMMENTS |
|----------|-------------|-----------|-------|--------|----------|
| 1 | Top | ¾" | 20" | 39" | |
| 2 | Stretchers | ¾" | 8¼" | 24½" | ½" TBE*; rabbeted for shelf |
| 1 | Shelf | ¾" | 14¾" | 23½" | Rabbeted for stretchers |
| 2 | Sides | ¾" | 16" | 29¼" | |

* Tenon both ends

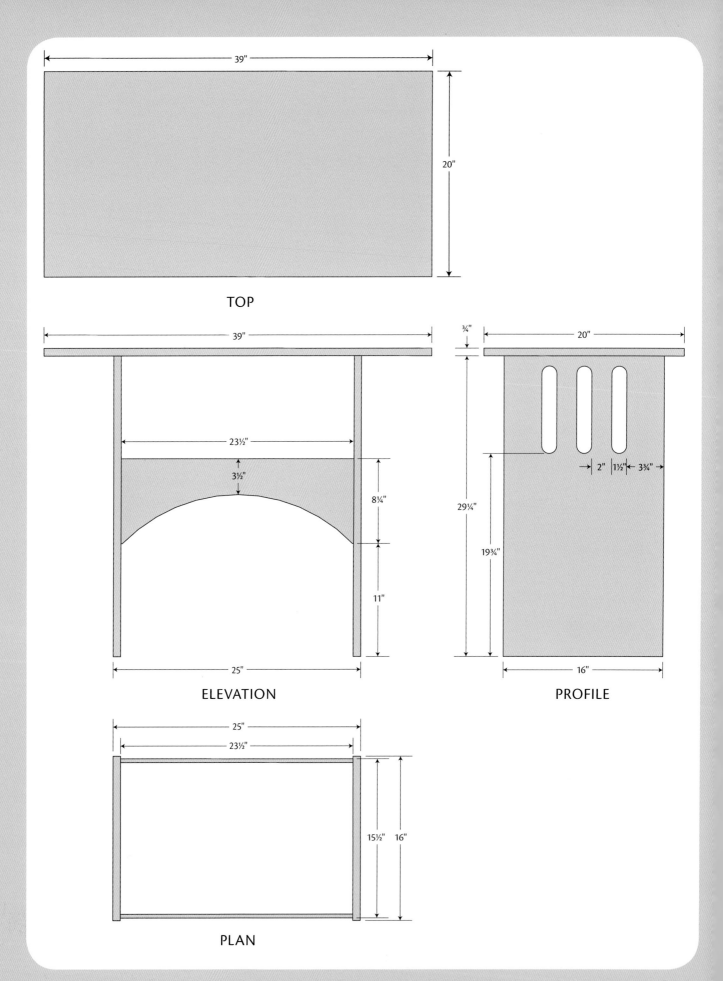

TOP

ELEVATION

PROFILE

PLAN

# SIDEBOARD

60" high x 62½" wide x 21½"deep
(1918)

ALTHOUGH IT BEARS some similarity to a sideboard designed for the A.S. Ball dining room in 1905, this unproduced design (possibly for Bassett-Lowke's Candida Cottage) dates from much later. The Italian firm Cassina prototyped it in 1973 and put it into production in 1974, with some changes to the drawings. The Cassina version omits a scalloped piece of trim from the top of the hutch alcove and doors on the compartments to the side of the alcove. It also substitutes a version of the Glasgow rose in stained glass for the mirror in the alcove. These drawings follow the Cassina version's omission of the trim piece to preserve the overall effect of an otherwise regimented geometric design.

Despite the scale of the piece, construction is relatively straightforward. The hutch and case are built separately and later combined. Mortise-and-tenon and dado joints predominate, with applied trim framing the drawers and doors.

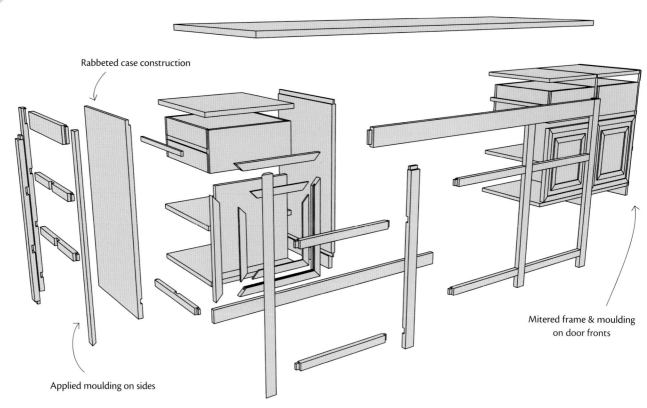

Rabbeted case construction

Mitered frame & moulding
on door fronts

Applied moulding on sides

## BASE, EXPLODED VIEW

# SIDEBOARD

| QUANTITY | DESCRIPTION | THICKNESS | WIDTH | LENGTH | COMMENTS |
|---|---|---|---|---|---|
| Base | | | | | |
| 3 | Bottoms | ¾" | 16³⁄₁₆" | 16¾" | |
| 2 | Dividers | ¾" | 16¾" | 29¼" | ¾" tenon top; dadoed for base bottom; notched for toe kick |
| 3 | Shelves | ¾" | 15¹¹⁄₁₆" | 16" | Use adjustable shelving hardware |
| 4 | Base drawer runners | ¾" | ¾" | 15" | |
| 2 | Outer base drawer runners | ⅜" | ¾" | 15" | |
| 1 | Case back | ½" | 27" | 50" | |
| 3 | Front bottom rails | ¾" | 1⅛" | 16" | ½" TBE* |
| 2 | Front inner stiles | ¾" | 1⅝" | 27⅛" | ½" tenon top end |
| 3 | Front middle rails | ¾" | 1⅛" | 16" | ½" TBE* |
| 2 | Front outer stiles | ¾" | 1⅝" | 29¼" | Mitered |
| 1 | Front top rail | ¾" | 2⅝" | 49¼" | ½" TBE* |
| 6 | Long inner door trim pieces | ¼" | 1⅛" | 11¼" | Mitered |
| 6 | Long outer door trim pieces | 1" | 1⅛" | 15¾" | Mitered |
| 3 | Lower door panels | ¾" | 13¼" | 14" | |
| 6 | Short inner door trim pieces | ¼" | 1⅛" | 10½" | Mitered |
| 6 | Short outer door trim pieces | ¾" | 1⅛" | 15" | Mitered |
| 2 | Side center stiles | ¾" | 1⅜" | 24½" | ½" TBE* |
| 4 | Side inner rails | ¾" | 1⅛" | 16¼" | ½" TBE* |
| 2 | Side lower rails | ¾" | 1⅛" | 16¼" | |
| 2 | Side outer stiles (front edge) | ¾" | 1⅜" | 29¼" | Mitered |
| 2 | Side outer stiles (back edge) | ¾" | 1⅜" | 29¼" | |
| 2 | Side panels | ¾" | 16¾" | 29¼" | |
| 2 | Side upper rails | ¾" | 2½" | 16¼" | ½" TBE* |
| 1 | Toe kick | ¾" | 2¼" | 48½" | Nailed or screwed in place |
| 1 | Countertop | ¾" | 21½" | 62½" | |

* Tenon both ends

| QUANTITY | DESCRIPTION | THICKNESS | WIDTH | LENGTH | COMMENTS |
|---|---|---|---|---|---|
| **Hutch** | | | | | |
| 1 | Center shelf | ¾" | 6½" | 30" | ¼" TBE*; curved front |
| 1 | Back panel | ¼" | 29⅝" | 50¾" | |
| 1 | Center rail | ¾" | 1⅝" | 29½" | Pocket hole screwed to case sides and tops |
| 2 | Door bottom rails | ¾" | 2⅛" | 7¼" | ½" TBE* |
| 2 | Door panels | ¼" | 7¼" | 20¾" | |
| 4 | Door stiles | ¾" | 1⅝" | 23½" | Grooved for door panel |
| 2 | Door upper rails | ¾" | 1⅝" | 7¼" | ½" TBE* |
| 2 | Drawer fronts | ¾" | 4¼" | 9½" | |
| 4 | Drawer long trim pieces | ¼" | ½" | 9½" | Mitered |
| 4 | Drawer short trim pieces | ¼" | ½" | 4¼" | Mitered |
| 4 | Cabinet bottom/horizontal dividers | ¾" | 9" | 9½" | ¼" TBE* |
| 4 | Cupboard shelves | ¾" | 8" | 9½" | Uses adjustable shelving hardware |
| 1 | Inlay square | ¹⁄₁₆" | 1½" | 1½" | |
| 14 | Inlay squares | ¹⁄₁₆" | 1½" | 1½" | |
| 2 | Sides | ¾" | 9½" | 30" | Rabbeted for back panel; dadoed for cabinet bottom & horizontal divider |
| 1 | Top | ¾" | 9½" | 50" | Dadoed for vertical dividers; rabbet for back panel |
| 2 | Vertical dividers | ¾" | 9" | 29⅝" | ⅜" tenon top end; dadoed for center shelf, cabinet bottom & horizontal divider |
| 1 | Mirror | ⅛" | 12" | 12" | |
| **Drawers** | | | | | |
| 3 | Base drawer backs | ½" | 6½" | 15" | Grooved for drawer bottom |
| 3 | Base drawer fronts | ¾" | 6½" | 15" | Grooved for drawer bottom |
| 3 | Base drawer bottoms | ¼" | 12¾" | 14½" | |
| 6 | Base drawer sides | ½" | 6½" | 15⅛" | Grooved for drawer bottom |
| 6 | Base drawer long trim pieces | ½" | ½" | 15" | Mitered |
| 6 | Base drawer short trim pieces | ½" | ½" | 6½" | Mitered |
| 2 | Hutch drawer fronts | ¾" | 4¼" | 9½" | |
| 4 | Hutch drawer long trim pieces | ¼" | ½" | 9½" | Mitered |
| 4 | Hutch drawer short trim pieces | ¼" | ½" | 4¼" | Mitered |
| 2 | Hutch drawer backs | ½" | 4¼" | 9½" | Grooved for drawer bottom |
| 2 | Hutch drawer bottoms | ¼" | 8¼" | 9" | |
| 4 | Hutch drawer sides | ½" | 4¼" | 8¼" | Grooved for drawer bottom |

Additional materials: 7 drawer pulls (see Hardware Resources, page 25)

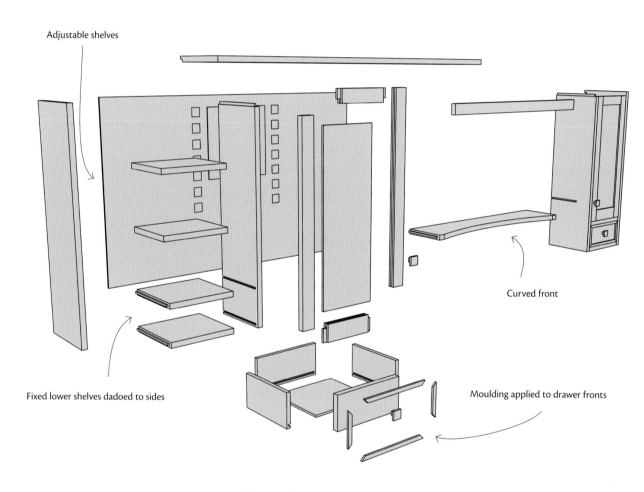

Adjustable shelves

Fixed lower shelves dadoed to sides

Curved front

Moulding applied to drawer fronts

HUTCH, EXPLODED VIEW

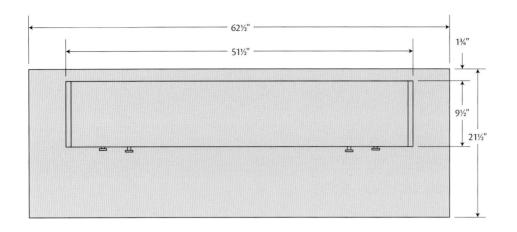

PLAN

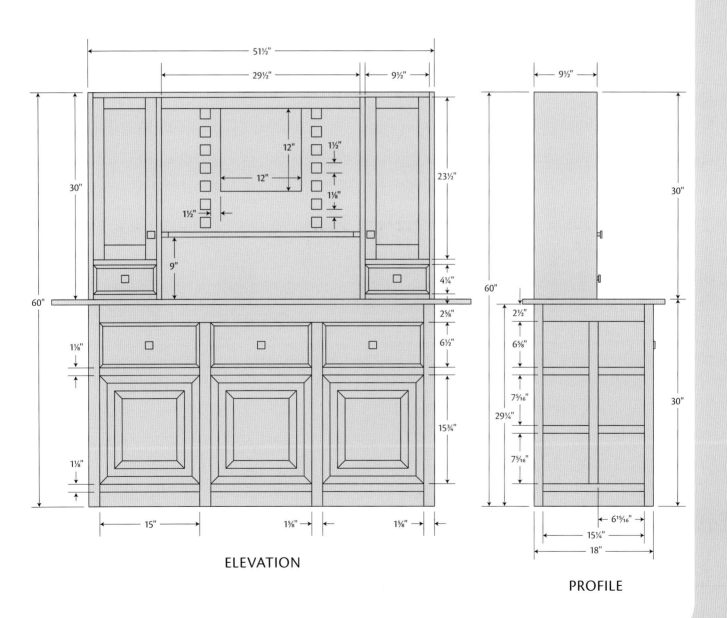

ELEVATION

PROFILE

# WILLOW TEA ROOM ARM CHAIR

28½" high x 21⅝" wide x 17½" deep
(1903), oak, stained dark

ALEXANDER MARTIN produced 50 copies of this chair in ebonized oak for the Willow Tea Room. The chair appeared in the ground floor Saloons, the Gallery and the Smoking Room. As with many of Mackintosh's other chair designs, the emphasis appears to be on form rather than function. A plain back relieved only by an arched cutout and front apron join two slab sides, with a minimal arm softening the edge of each tapered side. A lack of comfort hasn't lessened the chair's appeal; the Limbert Furniture Company appropriated the design for its No. 500 café chair in 1905. A pair of the original chairs sold at auction for £40,000 ($49,200) in 2016.

Sides screwed to back & seat

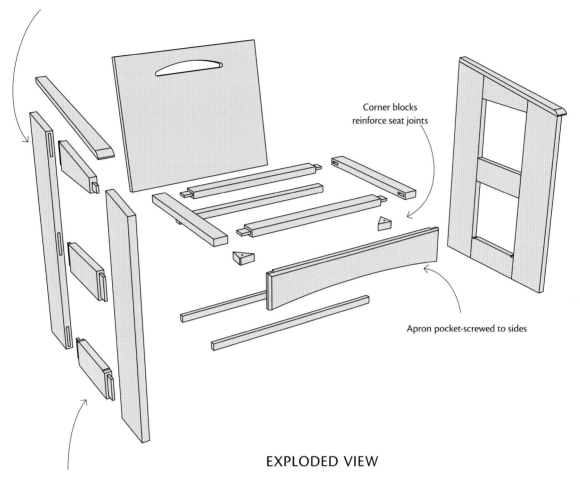

Corner blocks
reinforce seat joints

Apron pocket-screwed to sides

**EXPLODED VIEW**

Mortises & tenons join sides

## WILLOW TEA ROOM ARM CHAIR

| QUANTITY | DESCRIPTION | THICKNESS | WIDTH | LENGTH | COMMENTS |
|---|---|---|---|---|---|
| 2 | Arms | ½" | 1½" | 17¹⁷⁄₃₂" | |
| 1 | Back | ¾" | 18⅝" | 15½" | |
| 2 | Bottom stretchers | ½" | ¾" | 20⅛" | |
| 1 | Front apron | ¾" | 3½" | 20⅛" | Rabbeted for side short stile |
| 1 | Seat cleat | ¾" | 1" | 18⅝" | |
| 2 | Back legs | ¾" | 4¾" | 25¼" | |
| 4 | Middle/bottom leg rails | ¾" | 3" | 9¾" | 1" TBE* |
| 2 | Front legs | ¾" | 4¾" | 23" | |
| 2 | Side top rails | ¾" | 2¹⁵⁄₁₆" | 9¾" | 1" TBE* |
| 2 | Corner blocks | ¾" | 1¼" | 2⅛" | |
| 2 | Seat cushion frame stiles | ¾" | 1½" | 13¾" | |
| 2 | Seat cushion frame rails | ¾" | 1½" | 17⅝" | 1" TBE* |

* Tenon both ends

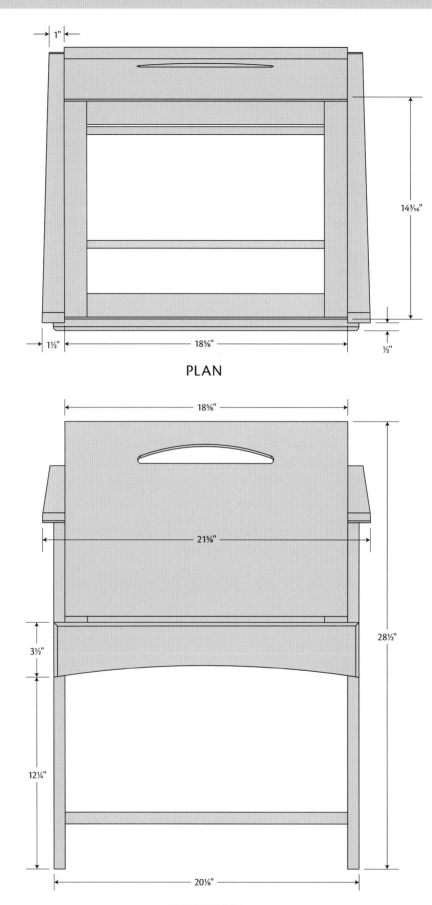

1"

14³⁄₁₆"

1½"   18⅝"   ½"

PLAN

18⅝"

21⅝"

3½"   28½"

12¼"

20⅛"

ELEVATION

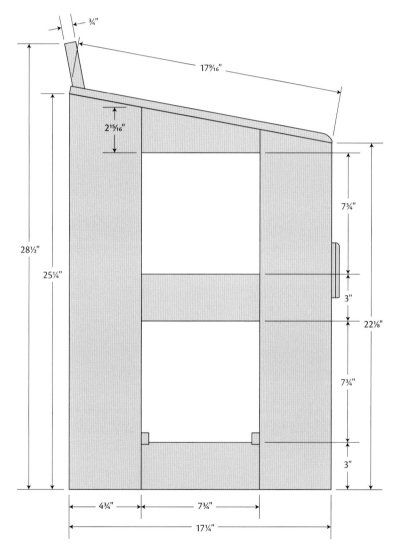

PROFILE

# CAFÉ TABLE

28" high x 60" wide x 24" deep
(1903), oak, stained dark

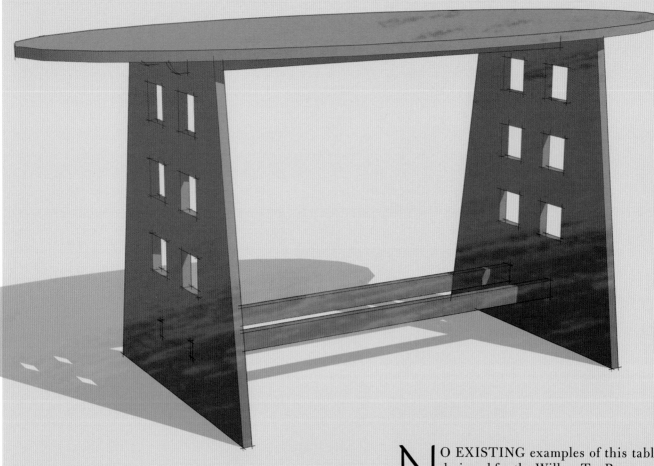

N O EXISTING examples of this table designed for the Willow Tea Room are known today, thus the drawings here are derived from a 1905 photograph (see page 15) of the Smoking Room featured in the German Art Nouveau magazine *Dekorative Kunst* and known dimensions of the chair also featured in the photograph. With its pierced, tapering slab legs and elliptical top, it bears some resemblance to the Hill House hall table (see page 108). The minimal design is quite flexible – vary the length of the stretchers and top to scale it up or down to suit your space. In the Tea Room, it was paired with the armchair (see page 94). The two make an attractive match for intimate dining.

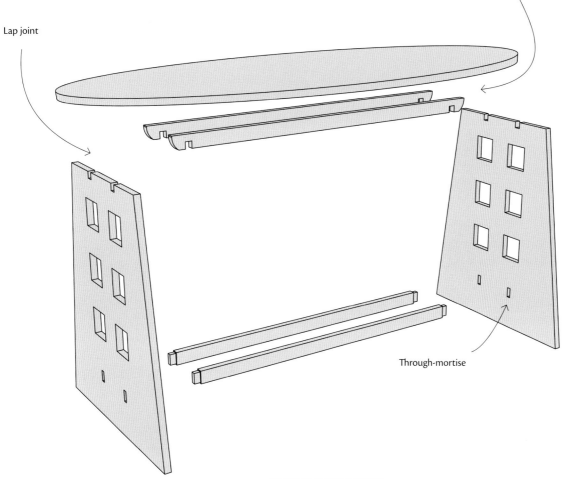

Lap joint

Stretchers screwed to top through elongated holes

Through-mortise

EXPLODED VIEW

## CAFÉ TABLE

| QUANTITY | DESCRIPTION | THICKNESS | WIDTH | LENGTH | COMMENTS |
|---|---|---|---|---|---|
| 2 | Legs | ¾" | 24" | 27¼" | Width tapers to 16" at top |
| 2 | Lower stretchers | ¾" | 1½" | 36" | ¾" TBE* |
| 1 | Top | ¾" | 24" | 60" | |
| 2 | Upper stretchers | ¾" | 1½" | 39" | |

* Tenon both ends

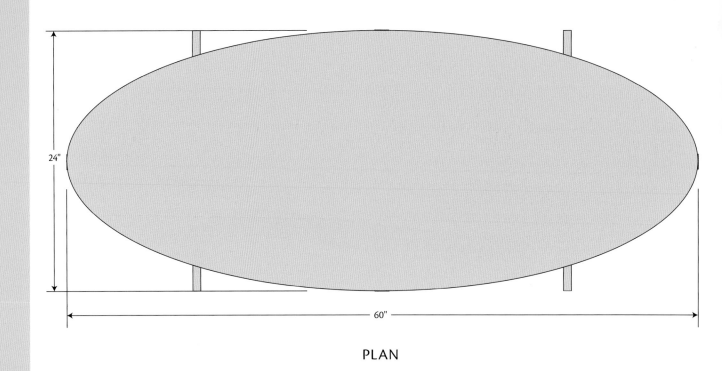

24"

60"

PLAN

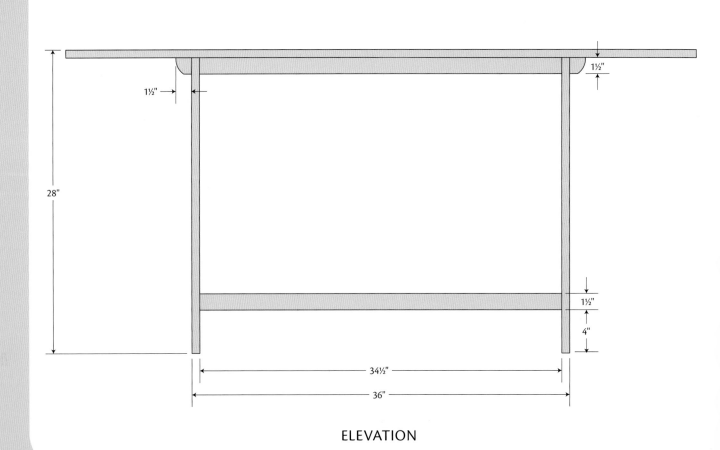

1½"

1½"

28"

1½"

4"

34½"

36"

ELEVATION

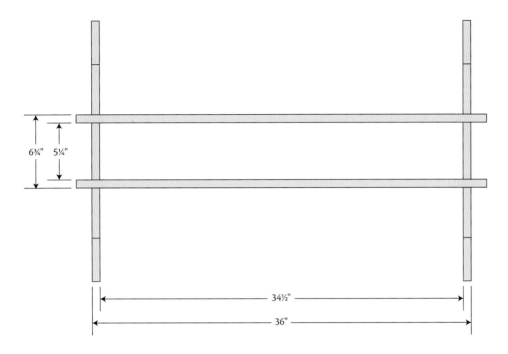

PLAN, SECTION VIEW, TOP REMOVED

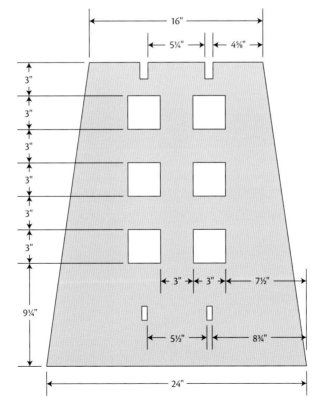

LEG PROFILE

# UMBRELLA STAND

56" high x 19" wide x 12" deep
(1904), ebonized pine

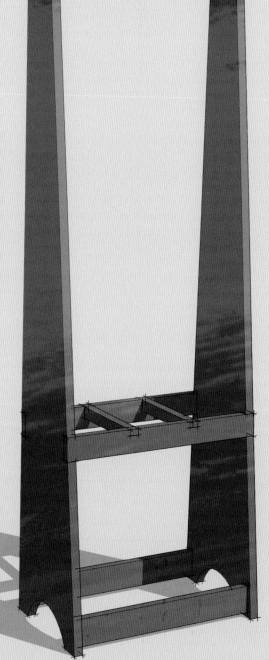

RATHER MODEST in design, this umbrella stand for the Hill House cloak room was built in ebonized pine. Two tapered sides are joined by rails at the top, middle and bottom, with dividers set every 5" in the upper rails to keep umbrellas separate as they air out. A chamfered top completes the stand. The drawings eliminate an additional bay to scale the piece for homes that weren't, unlike the Hill House, designed with a cloak room.

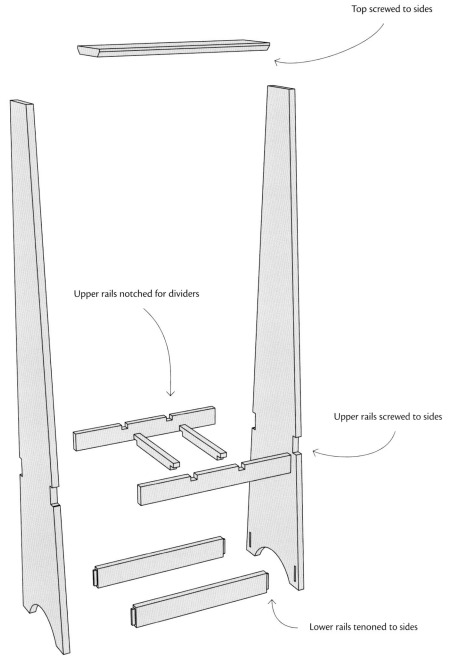

Top screwed to sides

Upper rails notched for dividers

Upper rails screwed to sides

Lower rails tenoned to sides

**EXPLODED VIEW**

# UMBRELLA STAND

| QUANTITY | DESCRIPTION | THICKNESS | WIDTH | LENGTH | COMMENTS |
|---|---|---|---|---|---|
| 2 | Sides | ¾" | 12" | 55¼" | |
| 2 | Lower rails | ¾" | 2⅜" | 17¼" | ⅜" TBE* |
| 2 | Upper rails | ¾" | 2" | 18" | |
| 2 | Dividers | ¾" | 1" | 9¾" | ¾" rabbet both ends |
| 1 | Top | ¾" | 5⅜" | 19" | ½" 45° chamfer along bottom edges" |

\* Tenon both ends

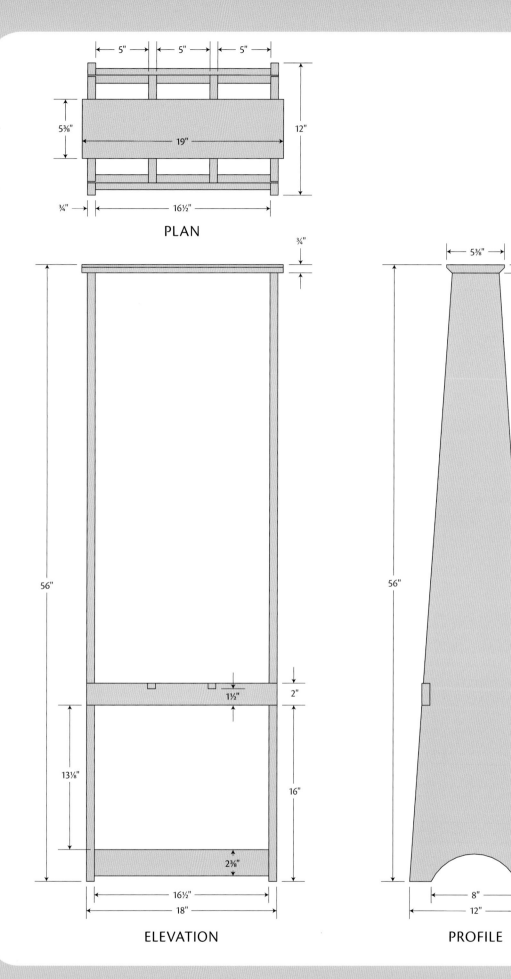

PLAN

ELEVATION

PROFILE

# MIRROR

66" high x 22" wide x ¾" deep
(1916), mahogany with mother-of-pearl inlay

BUILT BY PRISONERS-of-war at the Knock-
aloe camp on the Isle of Man, this mirror
designed for Bassett-Lowke shows the same
tendency for minimalism as other pieces Mackintosh designed for this demanding client. Gone are
the organic flourishes and extended supporting
structures of Mackintosh's earlier cheval mir-
rors. This design eliminates the stand and most
ornament – five inlaid squares of mother-of-pearl
provide the only decoration. Joinery is almost as
minimal as the design. Mortises and tenons join
the rails to the stiles, with the mirror set in rabbets.

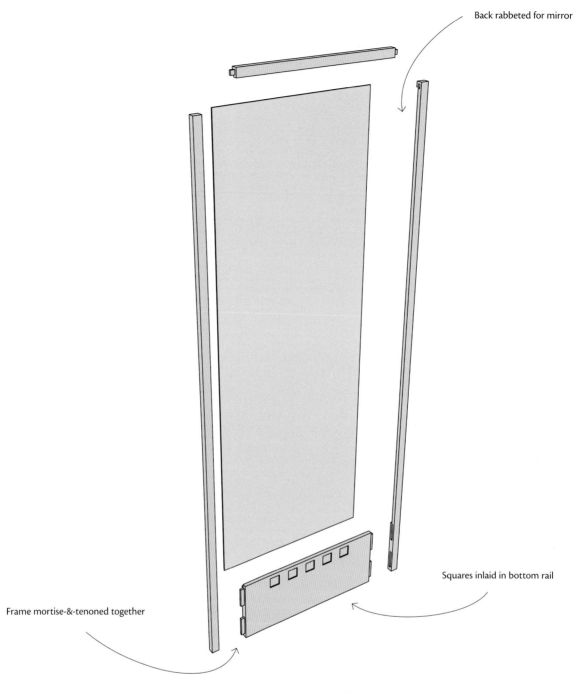

Back rabbeted for mirror

Frame mortise-&-tenoned together

Squares inlaid in bottom rail

**EXPLODED VIEW**

# MIRROR

| QUANTITY | DESCRIPTION | THICKNESS | WIDTH | LENGTH | COMMENTS |
|---|---|---|---|---|---|
| 1 | Top rail | ¾" | 1" | 21" | ½" TBE*; ⅜" rabbet for mirror |
| 1 | Bottom rail | ¾" | 8" | 21" | ½" double TBE*; ⅜" rabbet for mirror |
| 2 | Stiles | ¾" | 1" | 66" | ⅜" rabbet for mirror |

* Tenon both ends

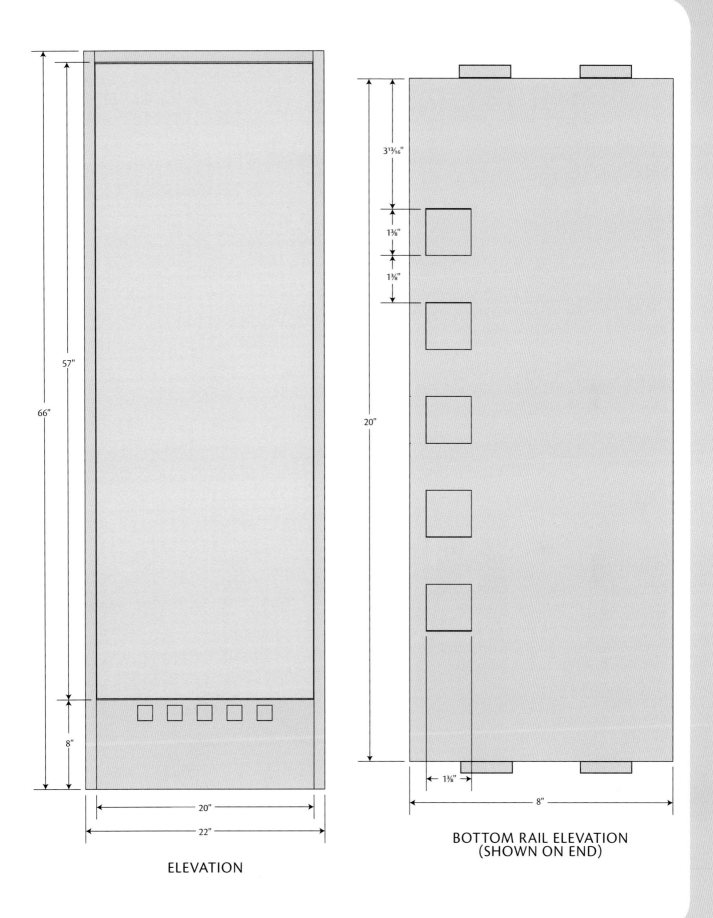

ELEVATION

BOTTOM RAIL ELEVATION
(SHOWN ON END)

# HILL HOUSE HALL TABLE

29" high x 60" wide x 30" deep
(1904)

THE HALL TABLE Mackintosh designed for Hill House shows the culmination of several different threads running through his designs for ovoid tables. Here the ends of the elliptical top have been cut short and the trapezoidal legs set under the table instead of along its perimeter. The cutouts provide the only ornament, their square shape echoed in the criss-crossing stretchers. John Craig was paid £7 ($897) to build the table.

The through-mortises and tenon joints may be the most challenging aspect of building the table with simpler mortise-and-tenon and lap joints predominating. The legs lend themselves to pattern routing, though the rounded corners a router bit produces will need to be squared. The drawer pull is a simple tapered turning.

Base screwed through elongated
holes in upper supports

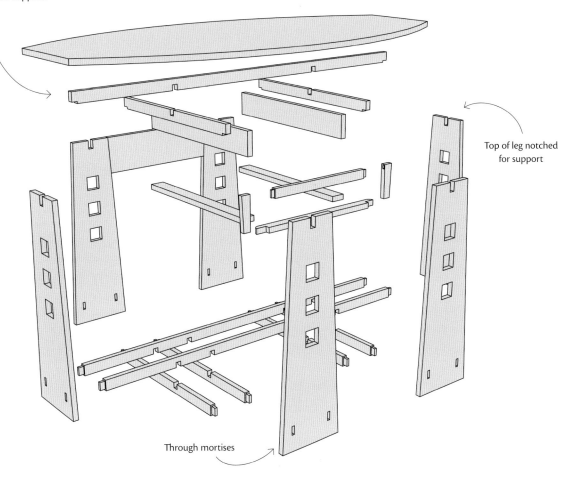

Top of leg notched
for support

Through mortises

**EXPLODED VIEW**

# HILL HOUSE HALL TABLE

| QUANTITY | DESCRIPTION | THICKNESS | WIDTH | LENGTH | COMMENTS |
|---|---|---|---|---|---|
| 6 | Legs | ¾" | 9" | 28¼" | |
| 2 | Lower long stretchers | ¾" | 1½" | 54" | ¾" TBE* |
| 4 | Lower short stretchers | ¾" | 1½" | 24" | ¾" TBE* |
| 1 | Upper long stretcher | ¾" | 1½" | 54" | |
| 2 | Upper short stretchers | ¾" | 1½" | 24" | |
| 1 | Top | ¾" | 30" | 60" | |
| 1 | Bottom face frame | ¾" | 1⅜" | 20½" | |
| 2 | Face frame stiles | ⅝" | 1⁹⁄₃₂" | 4¾" | |
| 1 | Top face frame | ⅝" | 1¼" | 16⁷⁄₁₆" | ½" TBE* |
| 1 | Back apron | ¾" | 5½" | 19½" | ¾" TBE* |
| 2 | Drawer rails | ¾" | 2" | 21¾" | Glued to drawer guides |
| 1 | Drawer front | ¾" | 3½" | 15⁷⁄₁₆" | |
| 1 | Drawer back | ½" | 3½" | 15⁷⁄₁₆"** | Grooved for drawer bottom |
| 2 | Drawer sides | ½" | 3½" | 11"** | Grooved for drawer bottom |
| 1 | Drawer bottom | ¼" | 10⁵⁵⁄₆₄" | 15⁷⁄₁₆" | |
| 2 | Drawer guides | ¾" | 3¼" | 22½" | Glued to upper short stretcher |
| 1 | Drawer knob | 1" | 1" | 1⅜" | |

* Tenon both ends

** Length varies based on joinery method

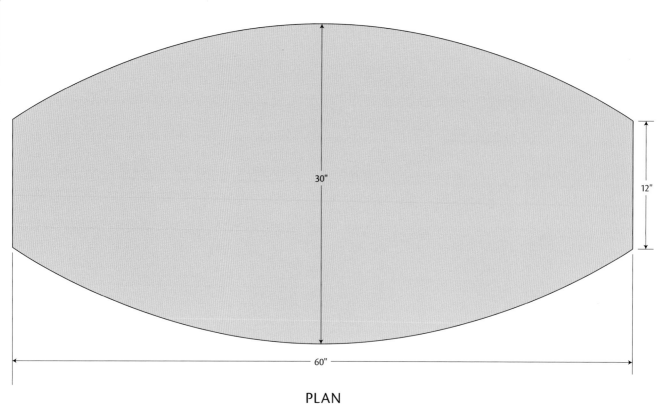

PLAN

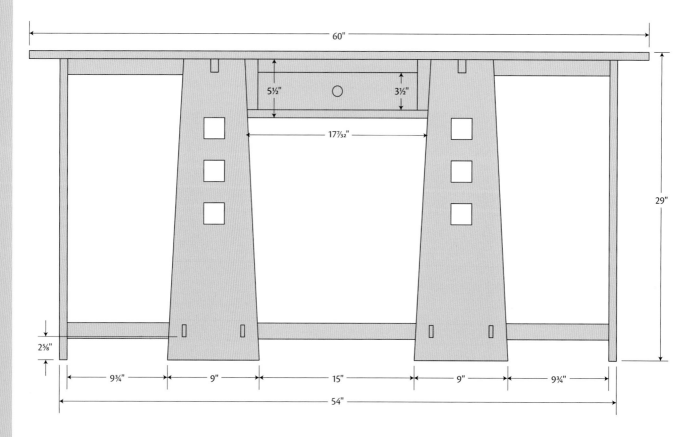

ELEVATION

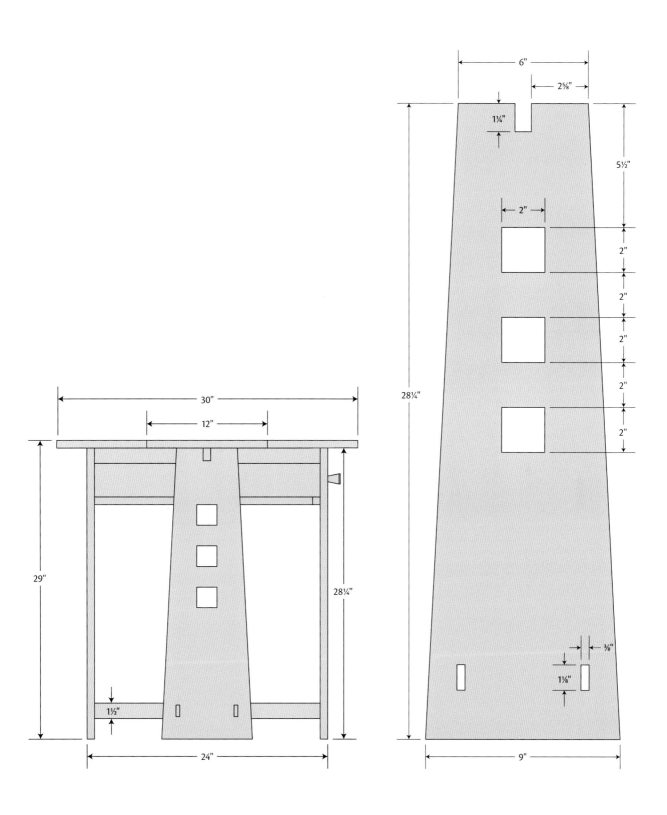

PROFILE

LEG PROFILE

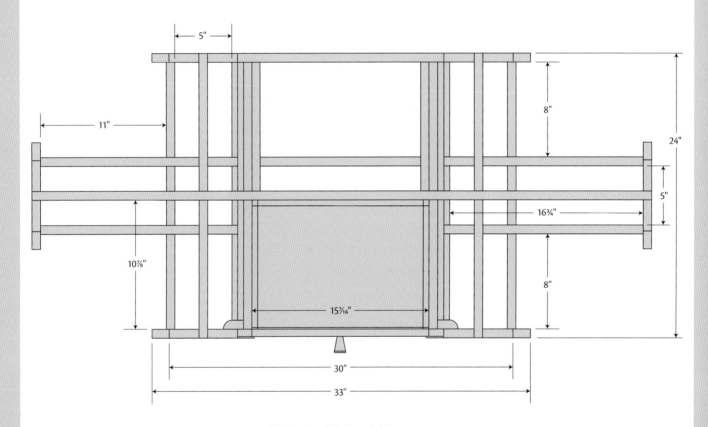

PLAN, TOP REMOVED

# HALL CHAIR

54¼" high x 26" wide x 21¼" deep
(1901), oak, stained dark

MACKINTOSH PROVIDES a unique interpretation of the gossip's chair in this piece designed for Windyhill. The curved back grants this hall chair an imposing grace. It also makes for a complex build. The back itself is coopered, with multiple boards forming the completed arc. It's also tapered, so the arms, apron and stretchers are cut at compound angles to meet it. Francis Smith was paid £2.64 ($342) each for a pair. A contemporary photograph shows one on either side of the hall's fire place (page 15).

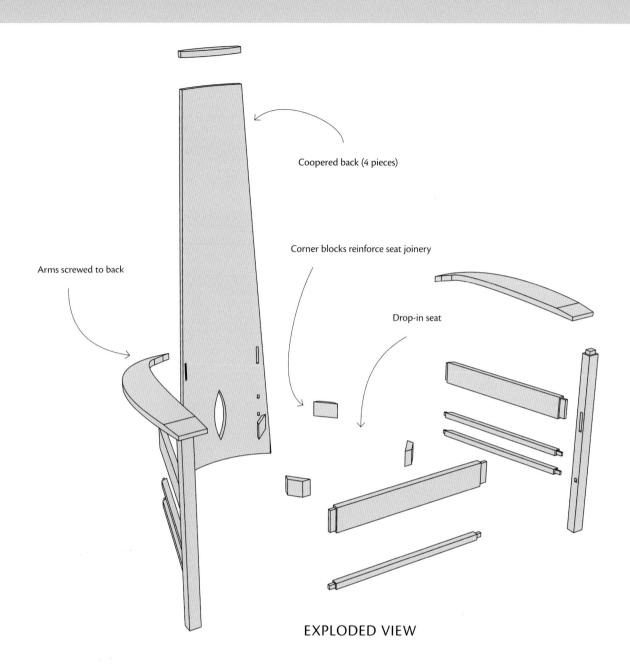

Coopered back (4 pieces)

Corner blocks reinforce seat joinery

Arms screwed to back

Drop-in seat

EXPLODED VIEW

# HALL CHAIR

| QUANTITY | DESCRIPTION | THICKNESS | WIDTH | LENGTH | COMMENTS |
|---|---|---|---|---|---|
| 2 | Arms | ¾" | 11" | 21¼" | |
| 1 | Back | ¾" | 14¹³⁄₁₆" | 53½" | Coopered panel; 4 pieces |
| 1 | Cap | ¾" | 2³⁄₁₆" | 8⅞" | |
| 1 | Front rail | ¾" | 3" | 21½" | ¾" TBE* |
| 1 | Front stretcher | ¾" | ¾" | 21½" | ¾" TBE* |
| 2 | Front legs | 1¼" | 1½" | 25" | ½" Tenon top end |
| 2 | Side rails | 3" | 5²⁷⁄₃₂" | 19" | ½" TBE* |
| 4 | Side stretchers | ¾" | 5¹³⁄₁₆" | 19" | ½" TBE* |
| 2 | Front corner blocks | 2" | 2⁷⁄₃₂" | 2¼" | |
| 2 | Rear corner blocks | 2" | 2¼" | 2¼" | |

* Tenon both ends

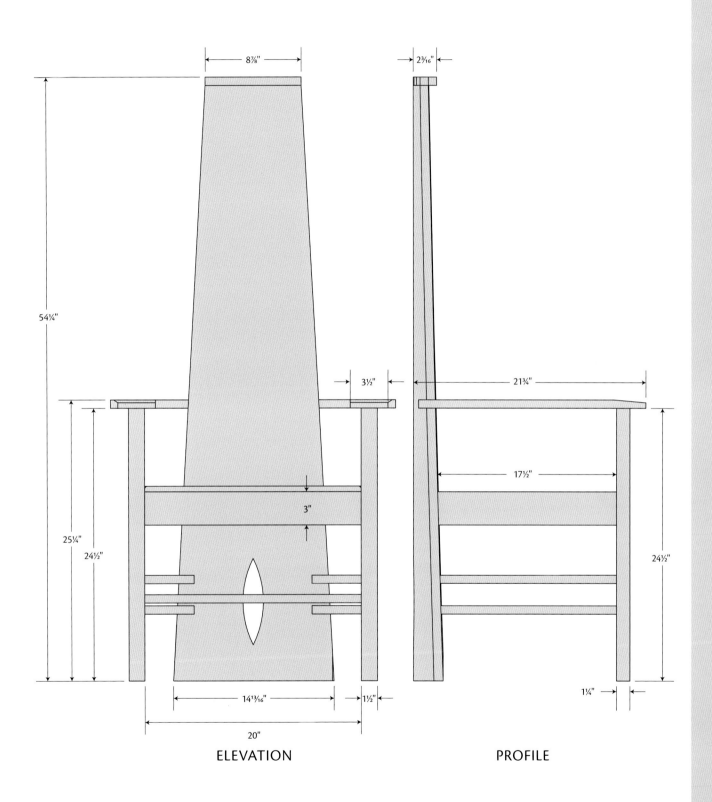

ELEVATION

PROFILE

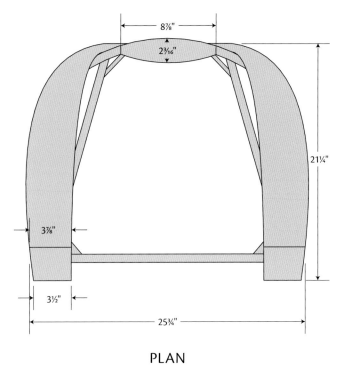

PLAN

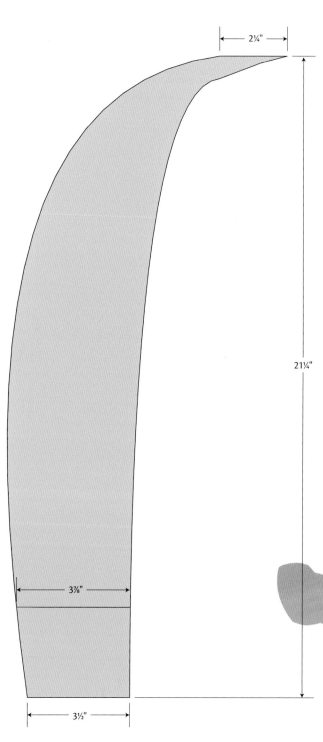

ARM PLAN

# SETTLE

23¼" high x 55" wide x 16" deep
(1900), oak

THIS SETTLE PROVIDES a seat for putting on shoes in an entryway or mudroom. The hinged seat also opens to reveal additional storage. It is a modest design originally intended for Mackintosh's own use. Rabbets and screws join the back and front to the sides, making the through-tenons set into the arms seem almost out of place. But anyone sitting on the bench is likely to enjoy the aesthetic touch this small embellishment provides.

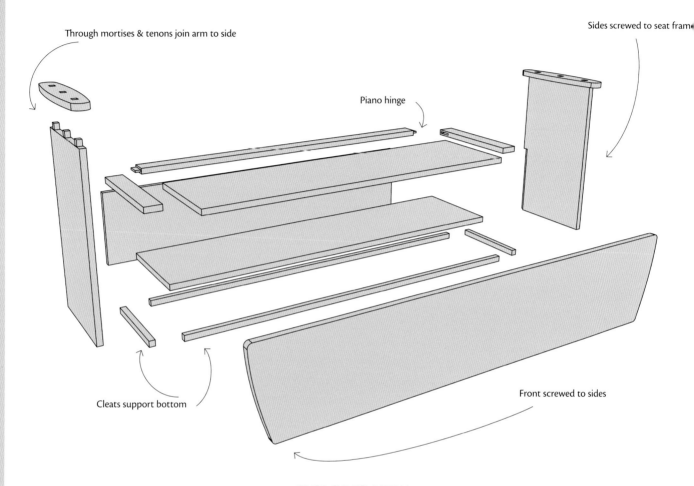

Through mortises & tenons join arm to side

Sides screwed to seat frame

Piano hinge

Cleats support bottom

Front screwed to sides

**EXPLODED VIEW**

# SETTLE

| QUANTITY | DESCRIPTION | THICKNESS | WIDTH | LENGTH | COMMENTS |
|---|---|---|---|---|---|
| 2 | Arms | ¾" | 3" | 16" | |
| 1 | Back apron | ¾" | 10½" | 50" | |
| 1 | Bottom | ¾" | 12¼" | 49" | |
| 1 | Front | ¾" | 10½" | 55" | |
| 1 | Seat | ¾" | 12¼" | 44½" | Hinged to back apron |
| 2 | Long cleats | ¾" | ¾" | 49" | |
| 2 | Sides | ¾" | 13" | 23¼" | ¾" tenons top end; rabbeted for back apron |
| 2 | Side cleats | ¾" | ¾" | 10¾" | |
| 1 | Seat rail | ¾" | 2¼" | 46" | ¾" TBE* |
| 2 | Seat stiles | ¾" | 2¼" | 14½" | |

* Tenon both ends

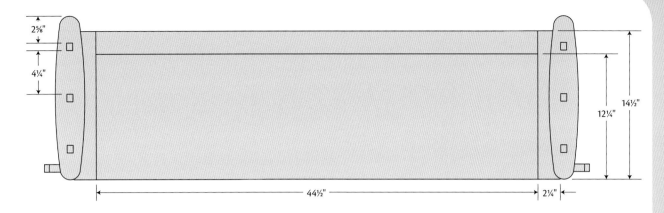

PLAN

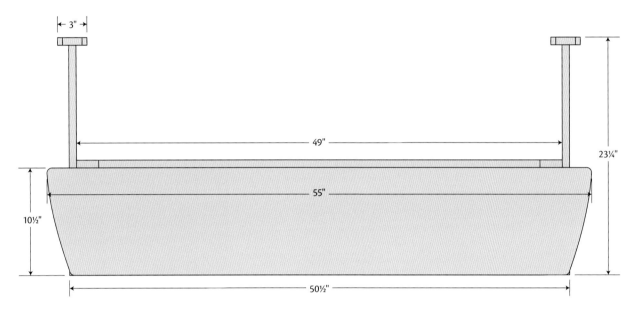

ELEVATION

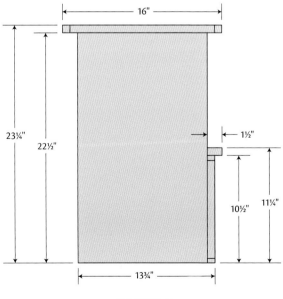

PROFILE

# WILLOW TEA ROOM CLOCK

74" high x 27½" wide x 6½" deep
(1903), oak, with steel face and brass markers

**D**ESPITE WHAT the tall case might suggest, this clock uses a movement that doesn't require a pendulum. Instead, display shelves occupy the case, with the door set into the lattice – an interesting alternative to having the door span the entire width of the case. David Hislop was paid £7 ($895) to build the clock for the Willow Tea Room. The latticed front and glass panels in the sides and back echo the square clock face, creating a precise, even rigorous, façade.

The design's precision calls for exacting construction. The sheer number of joints, despite the use of relatively simple lap joints and mortise-and-tenons, can be intimidating. Gang-cutting parts, or dadoing larger boards then ripping to width to produce multiple pieces, would expedite construction.

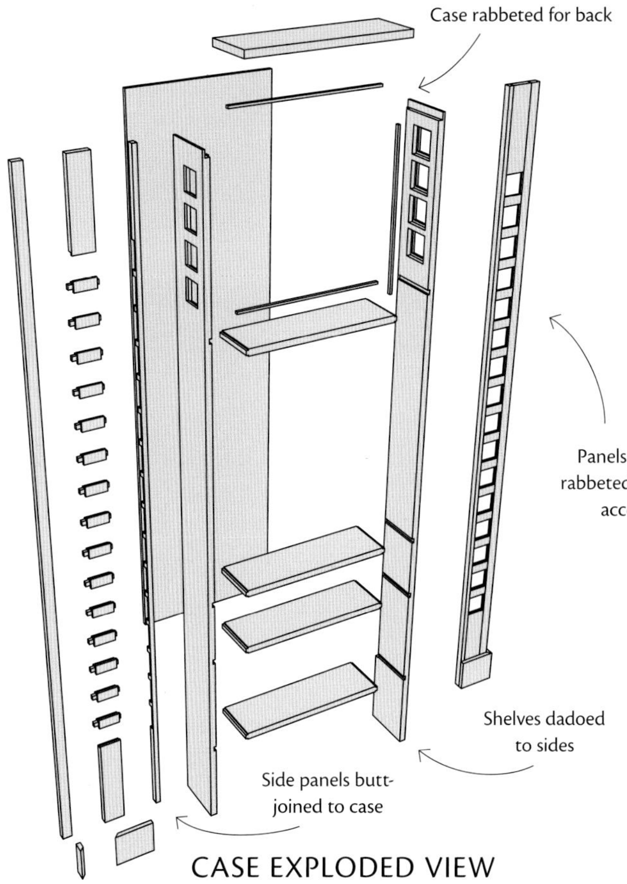
Case rabbeted for back
Panels & case rabbeted for glass accents
Shelves dadoed to sides
Side panels butt-joined to case

CASE EXPLODED VIEW

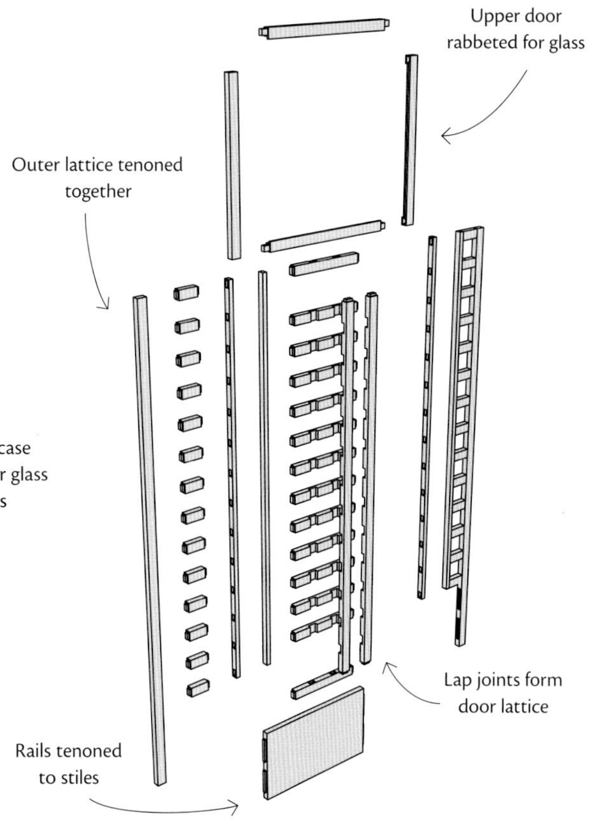
Upper door rabbeted for glass
Outer lattice tenoned together
Lap joints form door lattice
Rails tenoned to stiles

DOORS EXPLODED VIEW

# WILLOW TEA ROOM CLOCK

| QUANTITY | DESCRIPTION | THICKNESS | WIDTH | LENGTH | COMMENTS |
|---|---|---|---|---|---|
| 1 | Back | ½" | 17¾" | 64 15/16" | |
| 2 | Case sides | ¾" | 5¾" | 74" | Rabbeted for top & back; dadoed for shelves |
| 1 | Case top | ¾" | 5¾" | 18" | Rabbeted for back |
| 4 | Shelves | ¾" | 5¼" | 17½" | ¼" TBE* |
| 2 | Clock door rails | ¾" | 1⅛" | 17¼" | ½" TBE*; rabbeted for door glass |
| 2 | Clock door rails | ¾" | 1⅛" | 18½" | Rabbeted for door glass |
| 1 | Door glass | ⅛" | 16¾" | 16¾" | |
| 2 | Door inner stiles | ¾" | 1 3/32" | 45" | ½" TBE* |
| 12 | Door interior rails | ¾" | 1 3/32" | 9 5/16" | |
| 4 | Door outer stiles | 19/32" | ¾" | 46 3/16" | |
| 2 | Door outer rails | ¾" | 1 3/32" | 10 5/16" | ½" TBE* |
| 1 | Front bottom rail | ¾" | 9 5/16" | 17¼" | ½" TBE* |
| 2 | Front outer stiles | ¾" | 1⅛" | 55½" | |
| 40 | Glass inserts | ⅛" | 2⅞" | 2⅞" | |
| 2 | Long face supports | ¼" | ⅜" | 16 13/16" | |
| 2 | Long trim pieces | ½" | 3¾" | 4½" | Mitered |
| 2 | Short face supports | ¼" | ⅜" | 16½" | |
| 28 | Short rails | ¾" | 1 3/32" | 3⅛" | ½" tenon outside end; ¼" tenon inside end |
| 2 | Short trim pieces | ½" | 1¼" | 3¾" | Mitered |
| 2 | Side panel inner stiles | 17/32" | ¾" | 74" | |
| 2 | Side panel lower rails | ¾" | 10 13/32" | 2⅜" | Rabbeted for glass insert |
| 30 | Side panel muntins | ¾" | 1 3/32" | 3⅛" | ½" tenon outside end; ¼" tenon inside end; rabbeted for glass insert |
| 2 | Side panel outer stiles | ¾" | 1 3/32" | 74" | |
| 2 | Side panel upper rails | ¾" | 9 3/16" | 2⅜" | Rabbeted for glass insert |

* Tenon both ends

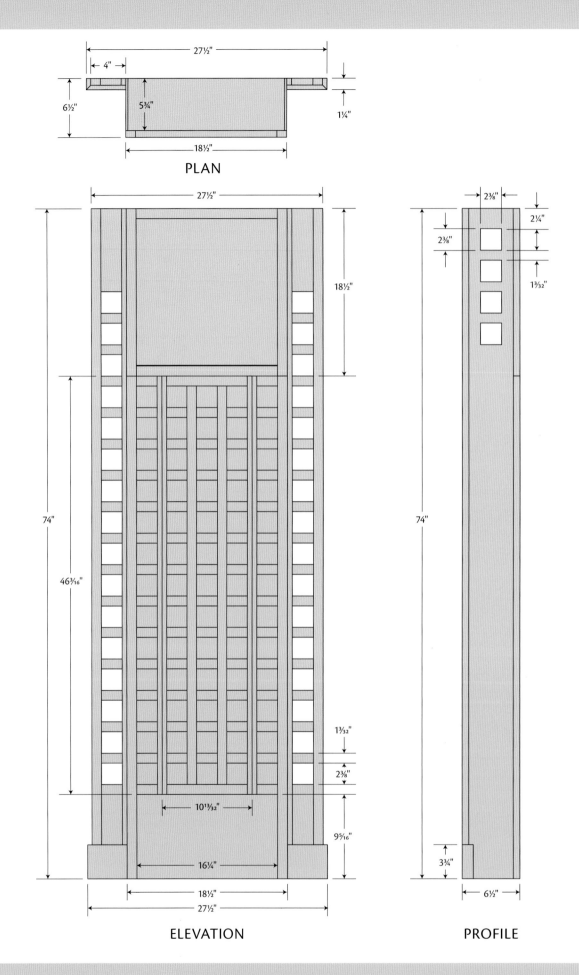

PLAN

ELEVATION

PROFILE

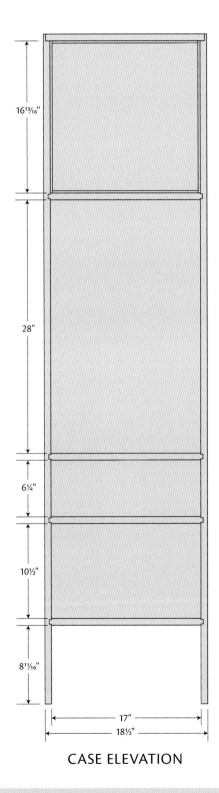

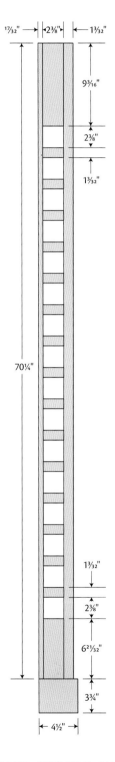

**CASE ELEVATION**

**RIGHT SIDE PANEL PROFILE, MUNTIN DETAIL**

# ARGYLE TEA ROOM SQUARE TABLE

27⅞" high x 23¾" wide x 23¾" deep
(1898)

ACCORDING TO Roger Billcliffe, Mackintosh first set the legs of a table based on a diagonal to the top with this design. It is a choice he returned to time and again. Here the decision may have been made to better showcase the carving, a stylized rendering of Ruskin's "head,

heart, hands," repeated on each face of every leg. Those carvings represent the most difficult aspect of the build. Lapped stretchers and a lower shelf join the legs, with the simplicity of the base further emphasizing the carving.

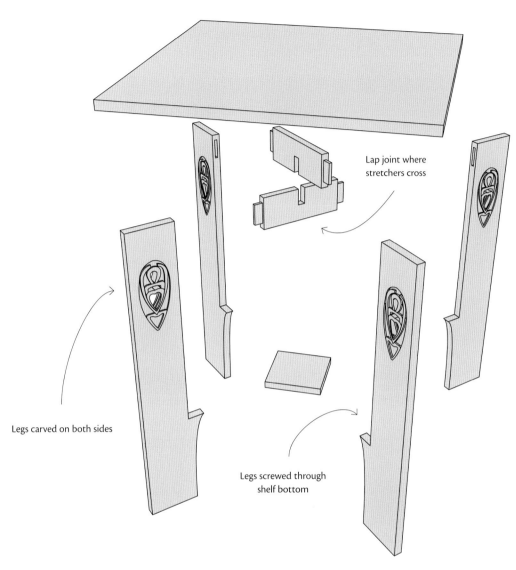

Lap joint where
stretchers cross

Legs carved on both sides

Legs screwed through
shelf bottom

**EXPLODED VIEW**

## ARGYLE TEA ROOM SQUARE TABLE

| QUANTITY | DESCRIPTION | THICKNESS | WIDTH | LENGTH | COMMENTS |
|---|---|---|---|---|---|
| 1 | Top | ¾" | 23¾" | 23¾" | |
| 1 | Shelf | ⅝" | 5⅛" | 5⅛" | |
| 4 | Legs | ¾" | 5⅝" | 27⅛" | |
| 2 | Stretchers | ⅝" | 2¾" | 8¾" | ¾" TBE* |

* Tenon both ends

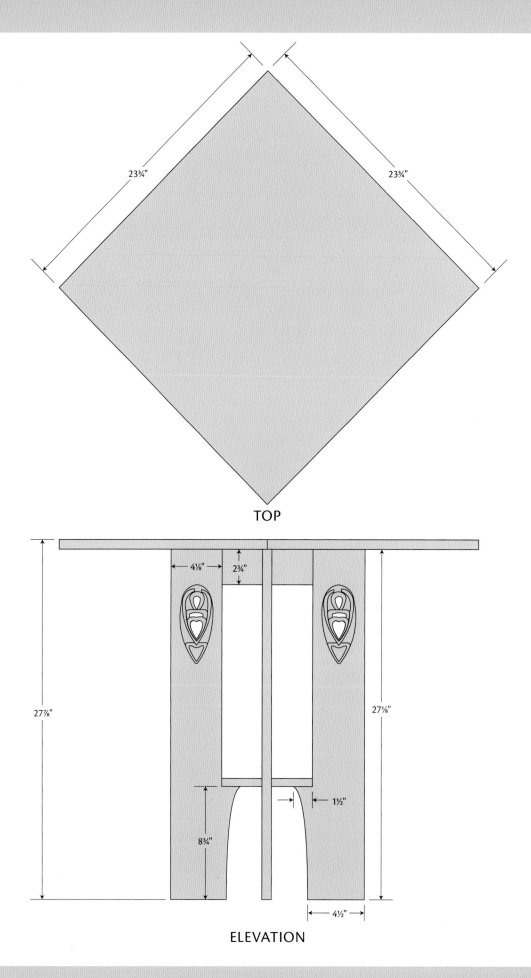

TOP

ELEVATION

23¾"  23¾"

4⅛"  2¾"

27⅞"  27⅛"

1½"

8¾"

4½"

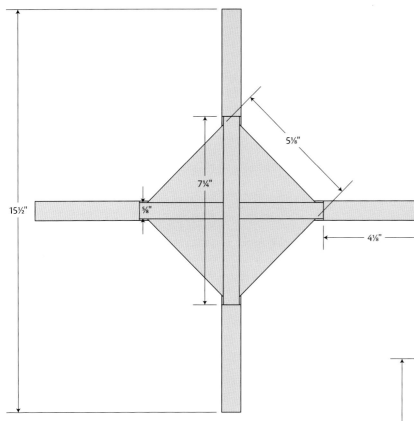

PLAN, SECTION VIEW

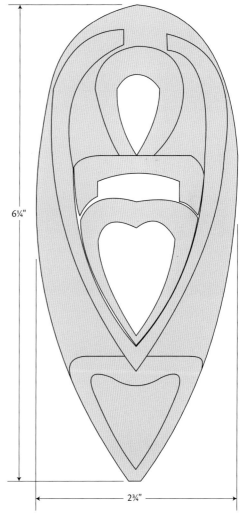

CARVING DETAIL

# CARD TABLE

26⅝" high x 24" wide x 24" deep
(1898), oak

BUILT FOR THE SMOKING Room of the Argyle Street Tea Rooms, this card table features an abstract carving in each apron. Although large, the carving's simple design makes it relatively easy to execute.

The tapered and canted legs present a minor challenge in geometry to bring the ends parallel to the floor.

A variation for this design also built for the Argyle Street Tea Rooms had a circular top, uncanted legs with a simple taper from the bottom of the stretcher on the inside faces, and a carving that did not pierce the wood. Another version for Mackintosh's home at 121 Mains Street had uncanted legs, pierced aprons, a square top and was painted white.

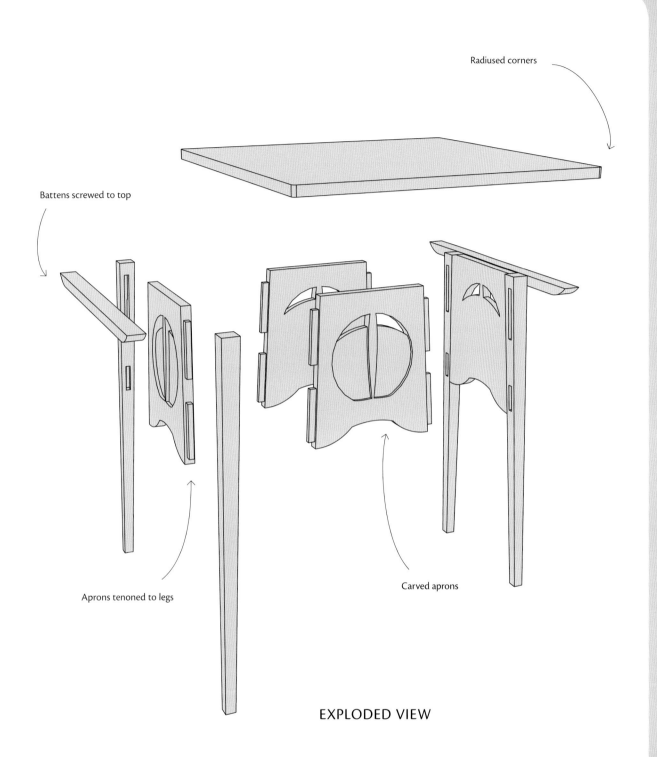

Radiused corners

Battens screwed to top

Aprons tenoned to legs

Carved aprons

**EXPLODED VIEW**

# CARD TABLE

| QUANTITY | DESCRIPTION | THICKNESS | WIDTH | LENGTH | COMMENTS |
|---|---|---|---|---|---|
| 1 | Top | ¾" | 24" | 24" | |
| 4 | Aprons | ¾" | 11¼" | 10½" | ½" double TBE* |
| 2 | Battens | ¾" | 1¼" | 21" | |
| 4 | Legs | 1¼" | 1¼" | 25⅞" | Tapers to ¾" x ¾" |

\* Tenon both ends

TOP

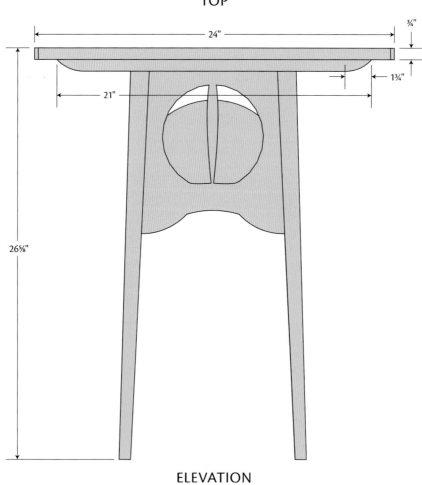

ELEVATION

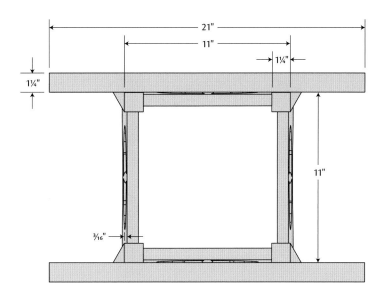

PLAN, SECTION VIEW

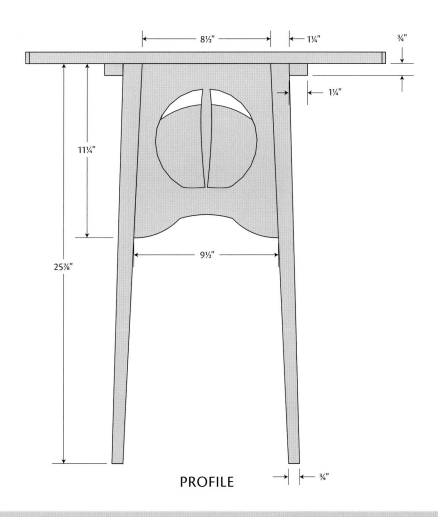

PROFILE

# HILL HOUSE DRAWING ROOM TABLE

25" high x 27" wide x 27" deep
(1908), ebonized pine with mother-of-pearl inlay

FROM THE MOTHER-OF-PEARL inlay, to the to repeating grid, to the shelves, to the top, the square dominates in this low table designed for the Hill House drawing room. At 25" high, it is too tall for a coffee table and too short for comfortable dining, but it would serve for cards or games. Alternatively, you could elimi-nate one row of the grid on the base, reducing the height to use the piece as a coffee table. Flanked by two high-backed chairs, as it is on display in the Hill House now, it forms an intimate conver-sational grouping within the expansive drawing room. Wylie & Lochhead were paid £7.15 ($887) for the table.

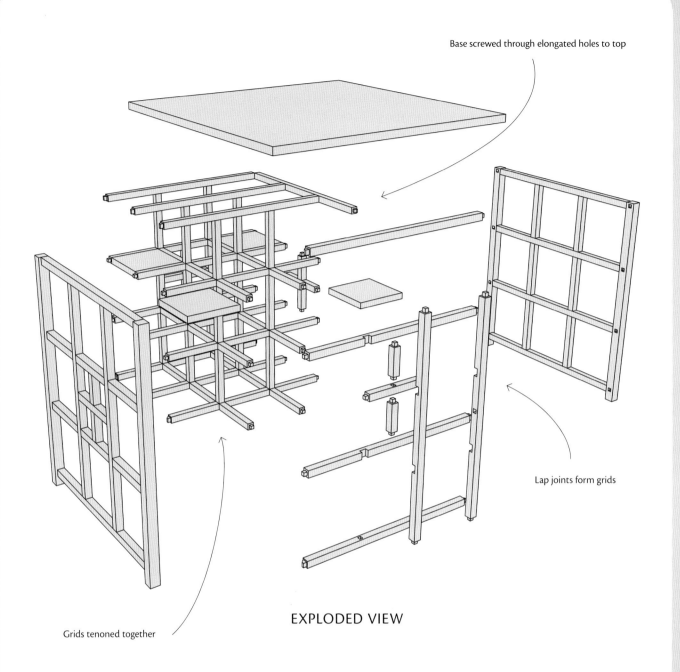

Base screwed through elongated holes to top

Lap joints form grids

Grids tenoned together

EXPLODED VIEW

# HILL HOUSE DRAWING ROOM TABLE

| QUANTITY | DESCRIPTION | THICKNESS | WIDTH | LENGTH | COMMENTS |
|---|---|---|---|---|---|
| 1 | Top | ¾" | 27" | 27" | |
| 4 | Legs | 1" | 1" | 24¼" | |
| 12 | Rails | ¾" | ¾" | 21¼" | ⅜" TBE* |
| 4 | Shelves | ¾" | 6⁵⁄₁₆" | 6⁵⁄₁₆" | |
| 22 | Horizontal crosspieces | ¾" | ¾" | 7¹⁄₁₆" | ⅜" TBE* |
| 12 | Stiles | ¾" | ¾" | 22½" | ⅜" TBE* |
| 12 | Stretchers | ¾" | ¾" | 21¼" | ⅜" TBE* |
| 8 | Vertical cross pieces | ¾" | ¾" | 3¾" | ⅜" TBE* |

* Tenon both ends

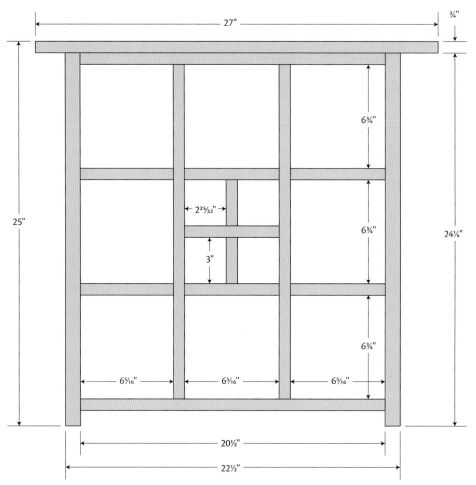

ELEVATION

27"

27"

TOP

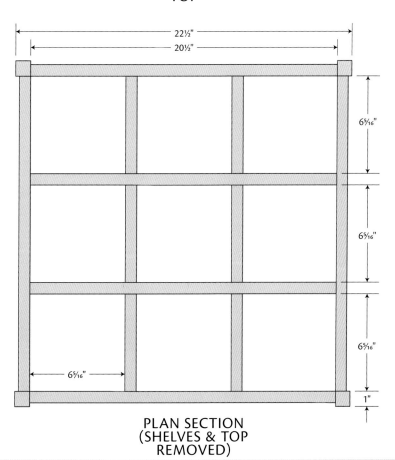

22½"

20½"

6⁵⁄₁₆"

6⁵⁄₁₆"

6⁵⁄₁₆"

6⁵⁄₁₆"

1"

PLAN SECTION
(SHELVES & TOP
REMOVED)

# DIACK BOOKCASE

53" high x 66½" wide x 15¼" deep
(1900)

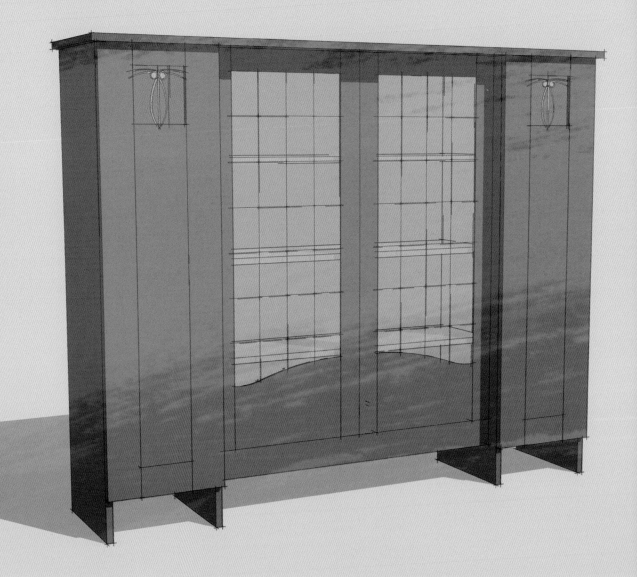

WITH ITS FLORIFORM leaded glass, curved lower rails in the doors and rectilinear form, this bookcase shows Art Nouveau and Arts & Crafts influences. Two smaller cabinets bookend a larger cabinet with inset, leaded-glass doors. The panels on the smaller doors are set flush with the outer center faces of the surrounding rails and stiles, rather than being set back. Unlike similar designs from the same era (including designs for Dunglass Castle and Mains Street), the base of this case is open, with the sides of the case extending past the bottom shelves to form slab legs.

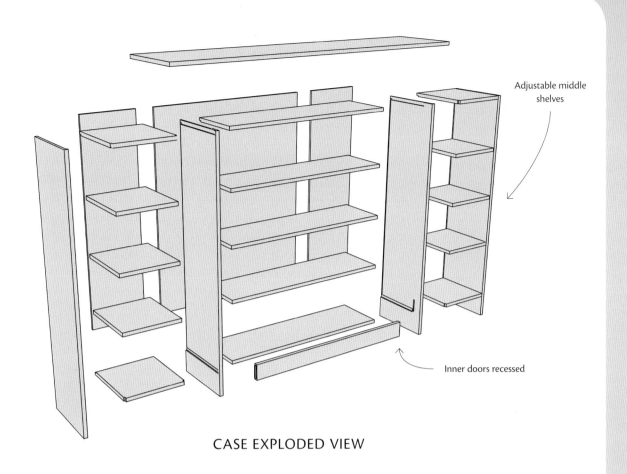

Adjustable middle shelves

Inner doors recessed

## CASE EXPLODED VIEW

# DIACK BOOKCASE

| QUANTITY | DESCRIPTION | THICKNESS | WIDTH | LENGTH | COMMENTS |
|---|---|---|---|---|---|
| 1 | Top | ¾" | 15¼" | 66½" | |
| 4 | Sides/vertical dividers | ¾" | 13¾" | 52¼" | |
| **Outer doors** | | | | | |
| 2 | Glass accent panels | ⅛" | 6½" | 6½" | |
| 2 | Bottom rails | ¾" | 3¼" | 8" | 1" TBE*; grooved for door panel |
| 2 | Door panels | ¾" | 6½" | 36¼" | ¼" tongue all around; top rabbed for glass accent panel |
| 4 | Stiles | ¾" | 3⅞" | 47½" | Grooved for door panel; rabbeted for glass accent panel |
| 2 | Top rails | ¾" | 2¼" | 8" | 1" TBE*; rabbeted for glass accent panel |
| **Inner doors** | | | | | |
| 2 | Door glazing | ¼" | 14¼" | 35³⁄₆₄" | |
| 2 | Bottom stretchers | ¾" | 9½" | 15¾" | 1" double TBE* |
| 2 | Rails | ¾" | 2½" | 15¾" | 1" TBE* |
| 4 | Stiles | ¾" | 2½" | 44¼" | |
| **Outer cases** | | | | | |
| 2 | Back panels | ½" | 12¾" | 46½" | |
| 6 | Shelves | ¾" | 12¼" | 13⅛" | |
| 4 | Short shelves | ¾" | 12¾" | 13¾" | Rabbeted for back panel |
| **Inner case** | | | | | |
| 1 | Long stretcher | ¾" | 3¼" | 38" | ¼" TBE* |
| 1 | Back panel | ½" | 38" | 46½" | |
| 2 | Bottoms | ¾" | 11¼" | 38" | Rabbeted for back panel |
| 3 | Shelves | ¾" | 10⅝" | 37½" | |

* Tenon both ends

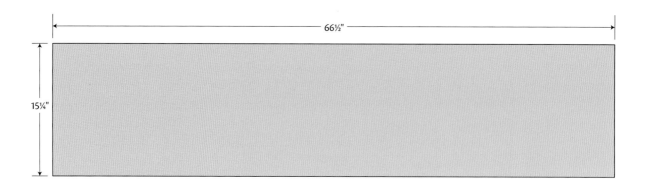

TOP

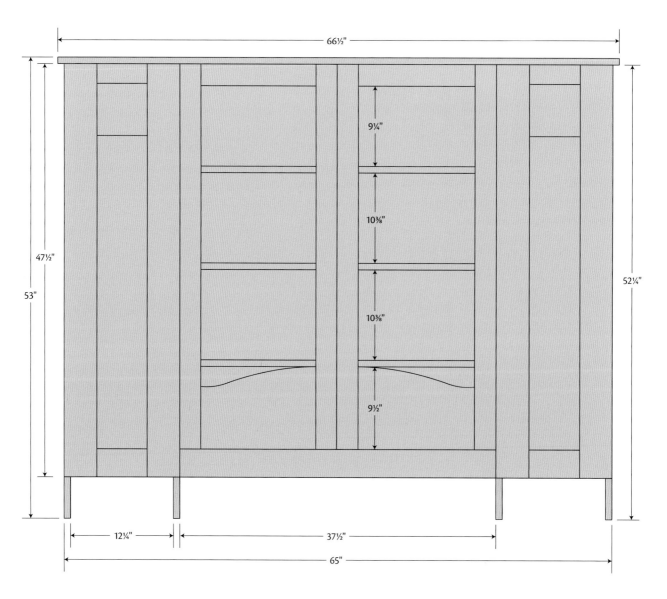

ELEVATION

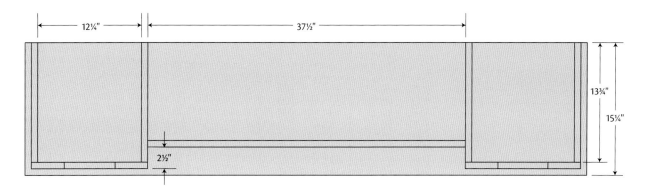

PLAN SECTION

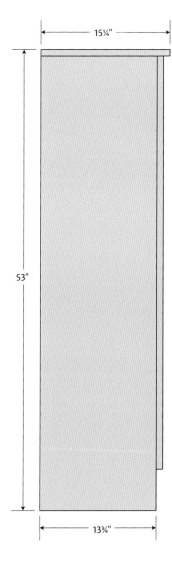

PROFILE

Rails & top of stiles rabbeted for glass

Rails tenoned to stiles

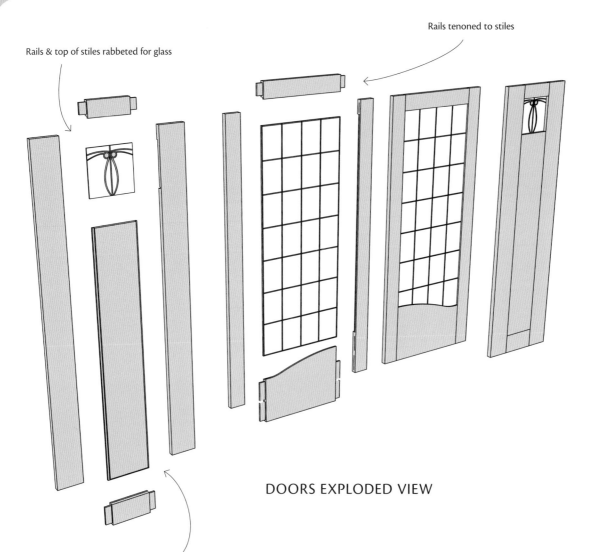

## DOORS EXPLODED VIEW

Rabbeted panels fit grooves in rails & stiles

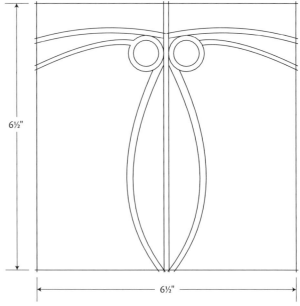

6½"

6½"

## GLASS PANEL

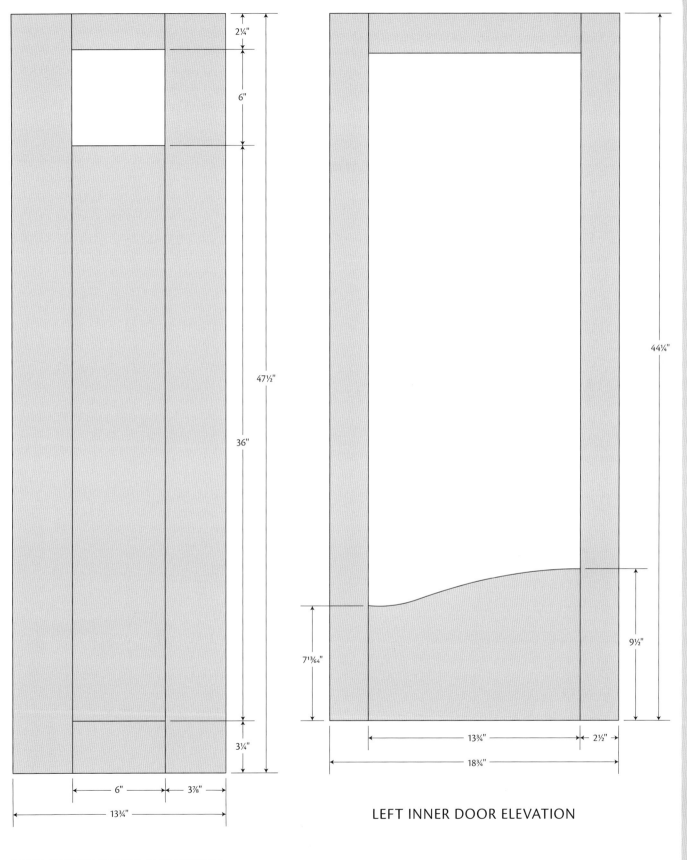

**LEFT OUTER DOOR ELEVATION**

**LEFT INNER DOOR ELEVATION**

# COUCH

19¼" high x 84" wide x 30" deep
(1910), birch, stained dark with gray corduroy cushion

BUILT FOR THE LADIES' Common Room in the Glasgow School of Art, this couch featured a back and upholstered arms in its original design. Fra Newberry's annotations on the plans suggest the substitution of loose cushions arranged against the wall for the back. It's not clear what drove the change, but cost may have played a role – Francis Smith quoted the original design at £8.25 ($966), the modified version at £6 ($744). Eventually moved from the Common Room to the Sculpture Room, the couch was accidentally set on fire and discarded. Salvaged by a student, it saw subsequent use as a stand for rowing sculls. Poor treatment did not diminish its appeal to collectors; at auction in 2013 it sold for $24,060.

Construction relies heavily on the mortise-and-tenon, the joint used to form the seat frame and to connect legs and arms to the seat. The large cushion is supported by either webbing or springs in a drop-in frame.

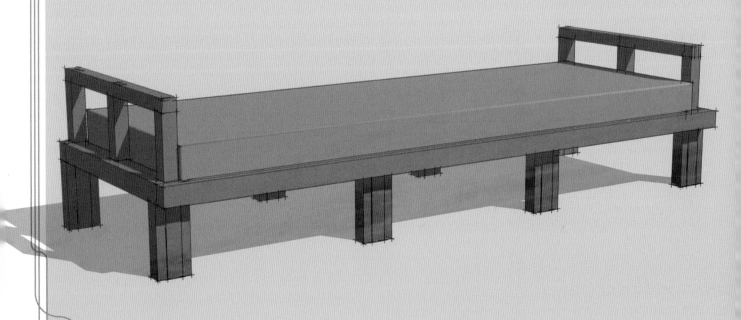

Webbing or springs in frame supports cushion

Cleats support seat frame

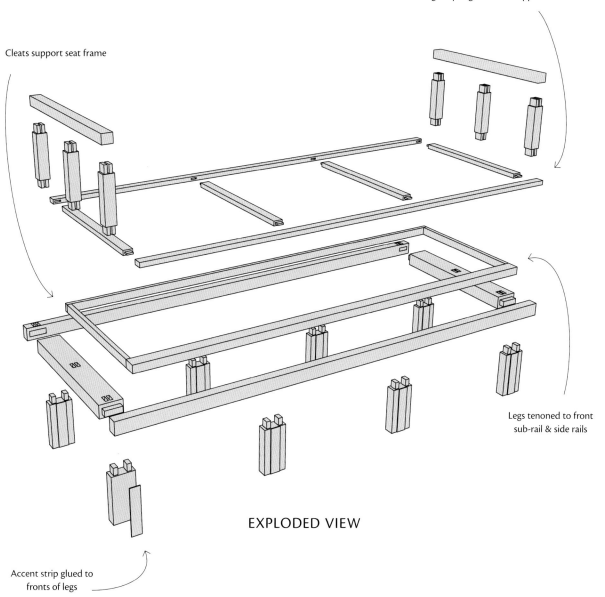

Legs tenoned to front sub-rail & side rails

Accent strip glued to fronts of legs

EXPLODED VIEW

# COUCH

| QUANTITY | DESCRIPTION | THICKNESS | WIDTH | LENGTH | COMMENTS |
|---|---|---|---|---|---|
| 2 | Arms | 1½" | 1¾" | 27¾" | |
| 6 | Arm supports | 1¾" | 1¾" | 9¾" | 1¼" double TBE* |
| 2 | Frame long rails | 1¾" | 2¼" | 84" | |
| 2 | Frame short rails | 2¼" | 4" | 28½" | 1" TBE* |
| 1 | Front subrail | 1⅜" | 2¼" | 76" | |
| 8 | Legs | 1¾" | 4" | 9½" | 1¼" double TBE* |
| 8 | Leg accent strips | ⅛" | 1¾" | 8¼" | |
| 1 | Long cleat | ¾" | 1⅜" | 76" | Glued & screwed to rails |
| 2 | Short cleats | ¾" | 1⅜" | 23½" | Glued & screwed to rails |
| 2 | Webbing frame rails | ¾" | 1½" | 76" | |
| 4 | Webbing frame stiles | ¾" | 1½" | 25" | ¾" TBE* |

* Tenon both ends

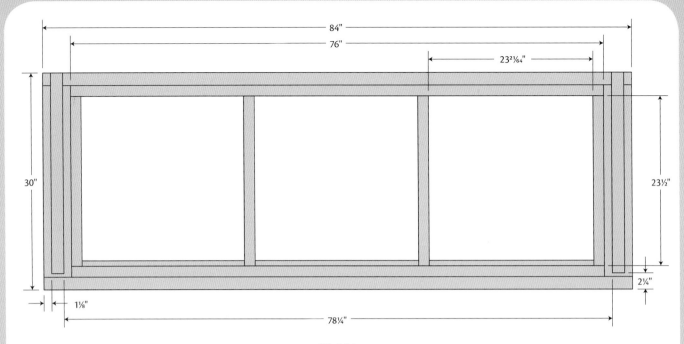

PLAN

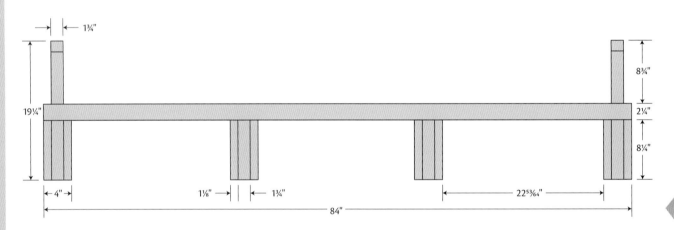

ELEVATION

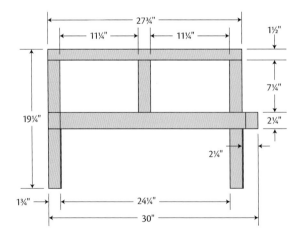

PROFILE

# OVAL TEA TABLE

24" high x 37" wide x 19" deep
(1902)

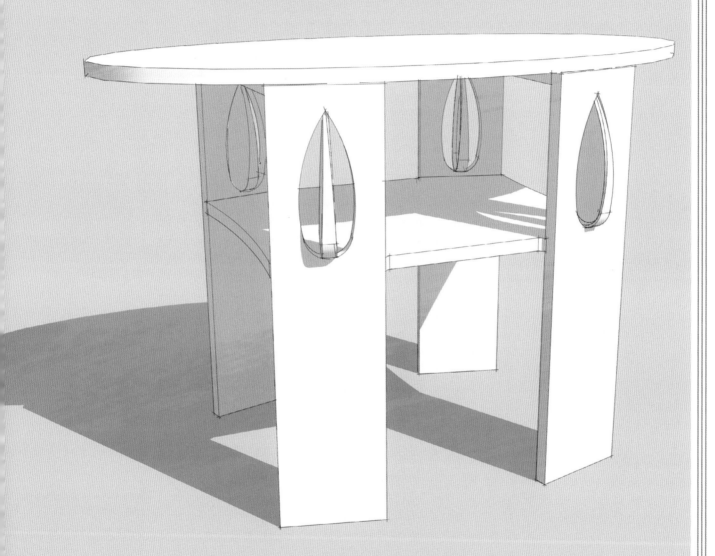

ORIGINALLY BUILT for Kingsborough Gardens, this design was later copied for exhibition in Turin, though the Turin version lacks the carved ivory panel inlaid in the earlier version. Four flat legs surround a shelf, and the top is anchored to the base through two stretchers, with the legs following roughly the curve of the elliptical top. A cutout in each leg frames a carved stylized flower.

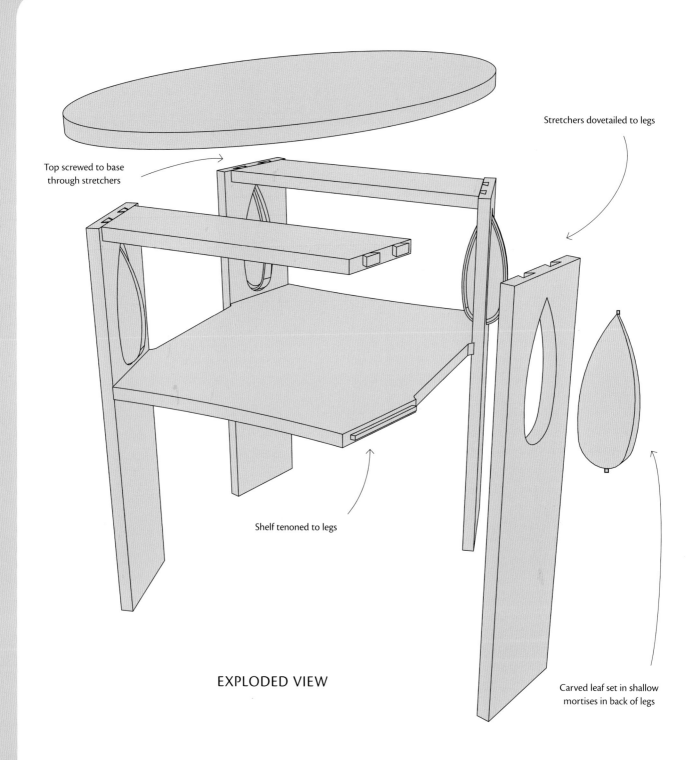

Stretchers dovetailed to legs

Top screwed to base
through stretchers

Shelf tenoned to legs

Carved leaf set in shallow
mortises in back of legs

EXPLODED VIEW

# OVAL TEA TABLE

| QUANTITY | DESCRIPTION | THICKNESS | WIDTH | LENGTH | COMMENTS |
|---|---|---|---|---|---|
| 4 | Legs | ¾" | 6" | 23¾" | Dadoed for shelf |
| 2 | Stretchers | ¾" | 5" | 18" | |
| 1 | Shelf | ¾" | 18" | 21⅝" | |
| 1 | Top | ¾" | 19" | 37" | |
| 4 | Cut outs | ¾" | 2¹⁵⁄₁₆" | 7¾" | Stub tenons both ends |

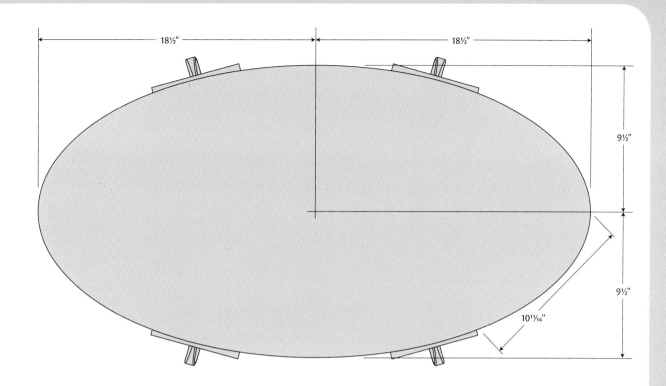

18½"    18½"
9½"
9½"
10¹¹⁄₁₆"

PLAN

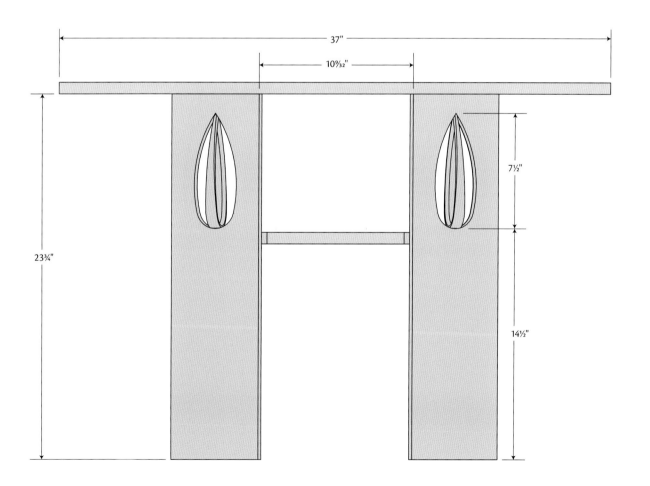

37"
10⁹⁄₃₂"
7½"
23¾"
14½"

ELEVATION

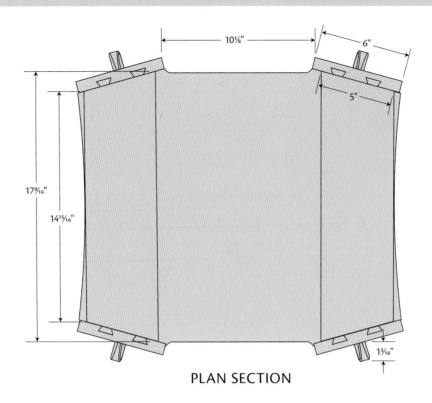

PLAN SECTION

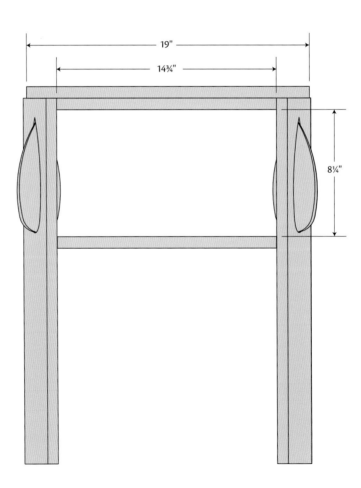

PROFILE

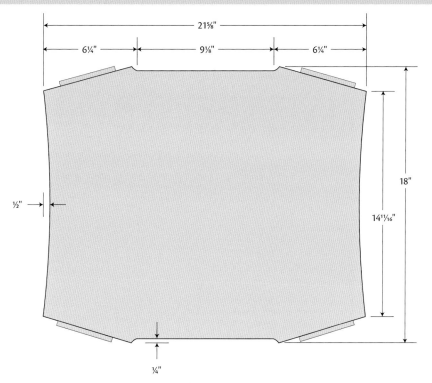

SHELF

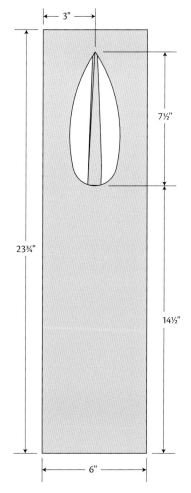

LEG DETAIL OUTSIDE VIEW

# MAINS STREET BOOKCASE

52" high x 109" wide x 12" deep
(1900), wood, painted white, and leaded glass

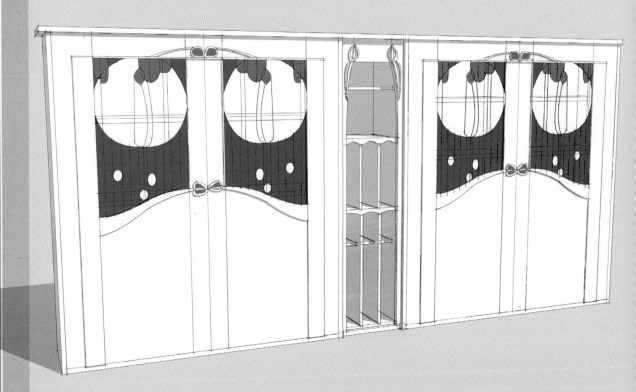

AS IN THE BOOKCASE for Michael Diack (see page 136), two enclosed cabinets flank a central case, with the center case set back. Unlike the Diack bookcase, this design for Mackintosh's own home at 120 Mains Street had two wider enclosed cabinets surrounding a narrower magazine stand. The design for the bookcase specifies it be built in three sections with the top then installed. While case construction is straightforward, the applied floral decoration requires some care.

# MAINS STREET BOOKCASE

| QUANTITY | DESCRIPTION | THICKNESS | WIDTH | LENGTH | COMMENTS |
|---|---|---|---|---|---|
| Outer Case | | | | | Parts yield two cases |
| 4 | Sides | ¾" | 12" | 51¼" | Rabbeted for back, top & bottom |
| 2 | Tops | ¾" | 11⁹⁄₃₂" | 47¼" | Rabbeted for back; dadoed for divider |
| 2 | Bottoms | ¾" | 12" | 47¼" | Rabbeted for back |
| 2 | Backs | ½" | 47¼" | 50½" | |
| 2 | Dividers | ¾" | 10¹¹⁄₃₂" | 50½" | ⅜" TBE* |
| 12 | Shelves | ¾" | 10¹¹⁄₃₂" | 22⅞" | Build additional as desired |
| 4 | Door bottom rails | ¾" | 16⅜" | 26¹¹⁄₁₆" | |
| 4 | Door inner stiles | ¾" | 3" | 50½" | |
| 4 | Door lower branch strips | ¼" | 6⅜" | 17¹³⁄₃₂" | |
| 4 | Door lower petals | ¼" | ½" | 2¹⁵⁄₃₂" | |
| 4 | Door narrow trim pieces | ¼" | ¼" | 20⁹⁄₆₄" | |
| 4 | Door outer stiles | ¾" | 5⅞" | 50½" | |
| 4 | Door upper blossoms | ¼" | 1¾" | 2⁷⁄₃₂" | |
| 4 | Door upper petals | ¼" | 1⅛" | 2⁷⁄₁₆" | |
| 4 | Door upper rails | ¾" | 3½" | 16⅜" | 1" TBE* |
| 4 | Door upper trim pieces | ¼" | ¼" | 20¹³⁄₃₂" | |
| 4 | Door upper vines | ¼" | 1½" | 7⅜" | |
| 4 | Door wide accent strips | ¼" | 3" | 46²⁷⁄₃₂" | |
| Center Case | | | | | |
| 2 | Sides | ¾" | 10²⁵⁄₃₂" | 51¼" | |
| 1 | Top | ¾" | 10⁵¹⁄₆₄" | 11¼" | Rabbeted for back |
| 1 | Bottom | ¾" | 11¼" | 11½" | |
| 1 | Back | ½" | 11¼" | 50⅛" | |
| 1 | Arced shelf edge band | ½" | 1" | 10½" | |
| 1 | Scalloped shelf edge trim | ½" | 1" | 10½" | |
| 2 | Long dividers | ½" | 10⁵⁄₁₆" | 20¹⁹⁄₃₂" | ⅛" TBE* |
| 2 | Dividers | ½" | 9¹³⁄₁₆" | 12¹⁄₁₆" | ⅛" TBE* |
| 2 | Face frame stiles | ¾" | 2⅜" | 51¼" | |
| 1 | Face frame top rail | ¾" | 3²⁷⁄₃₂" | 8¾" | ¾" TBE* |
| 2 | Flower accents | ¼" | 2⁵⁄₁₆" | 9⅛" | |
| 1 | Shallow shelf | ½" | 8¹¹⁄₃₂" | 10¾" | ⅛" TBE* |
| 1 | Bottom shelf | ½" | 10⁵⁄₁₆" | 10½" | Dadoed for dividers |
| 2 | Intermediate shelves | ½" | 9¹³⁄₁₆" | 10¾" | Dadoed for dividers |
| 1 | Shelf center section | ½" | 3⅜" | 8⁵⁄₁₆" | |
| 2 | Shelf outer sections | ½" | 3⁷⁄₁₆" | 8⁵⁄₁₆" | |
| Top | | | | | |
| 1 | Top | ¾" | 12½" | 109" | |

*Tenon both ends

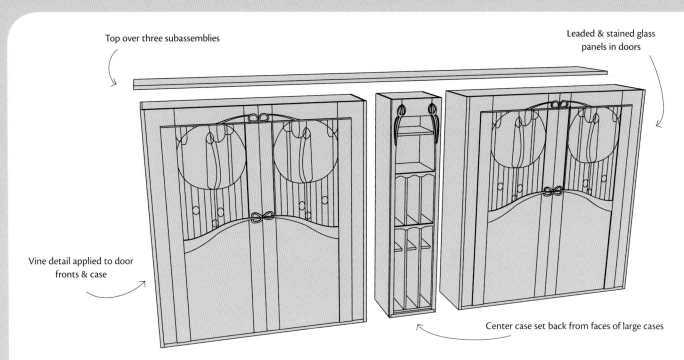

Top over three subassemblies

Leaded & stained glass panels in doors

Vine detail applied to door fronts & case

Center case set back from faces of large cases

**SUBASSEMBLIES**

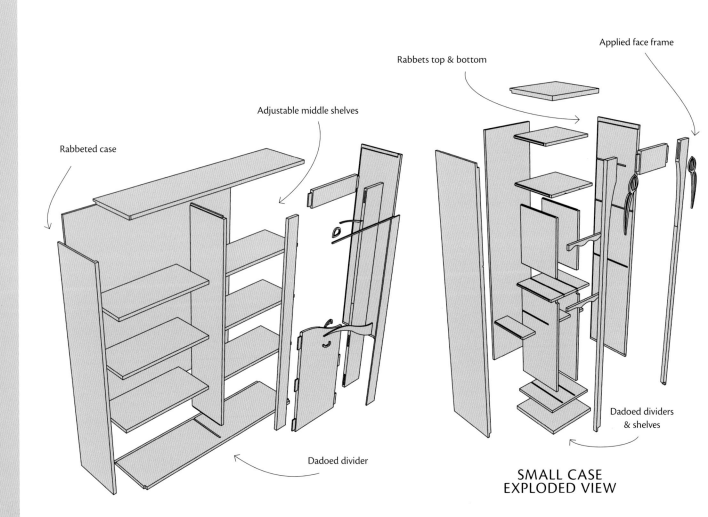

Rabbets top & bottom

Applied face frame

Adjustable middle shelves

Rabbeted case

Dadoed dividers & shelves

Dadoed divider

**SMALL CASE EXPLODED VIEW**

**LARGE CASE EXPLODED VIEW (ONE DOOR REMOVED)**

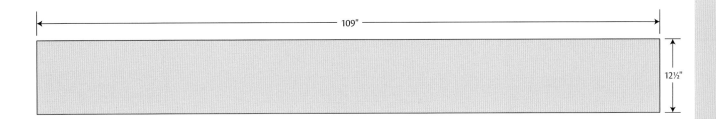

109"

12½"

TOP

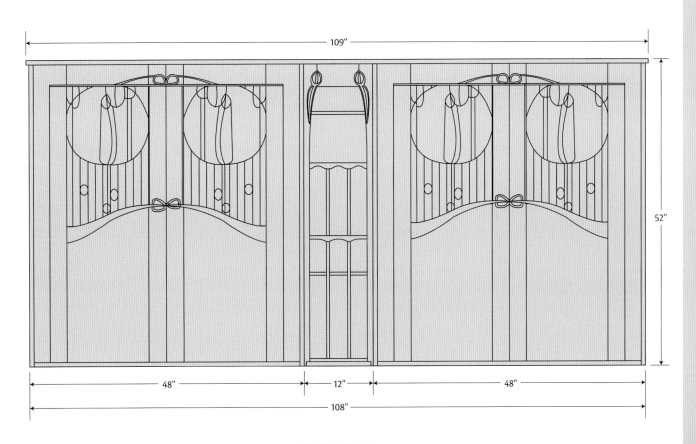

109"

52"

48"  12"  48"

108"

ELEVATION

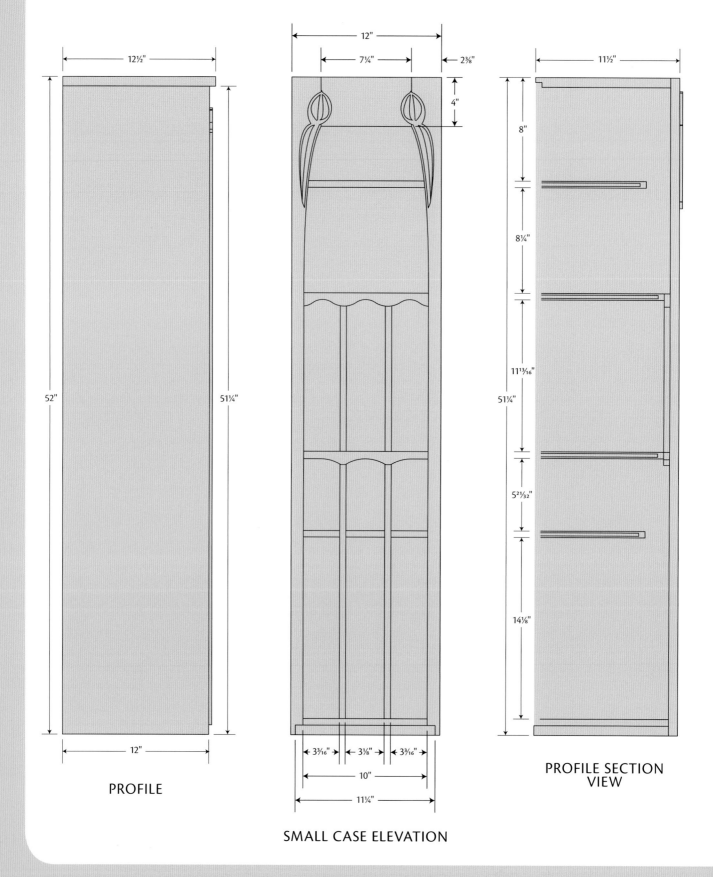

PROFILE

SMALL CASE ELEVATION

PROFILE SECTION
VIEW

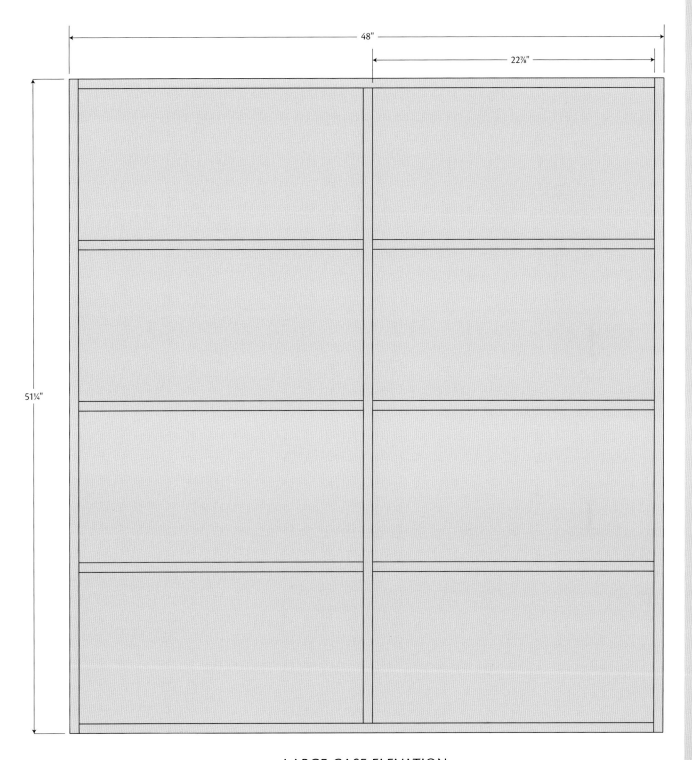

LARGE CASE ELEVATION,
DOORS REMOVED

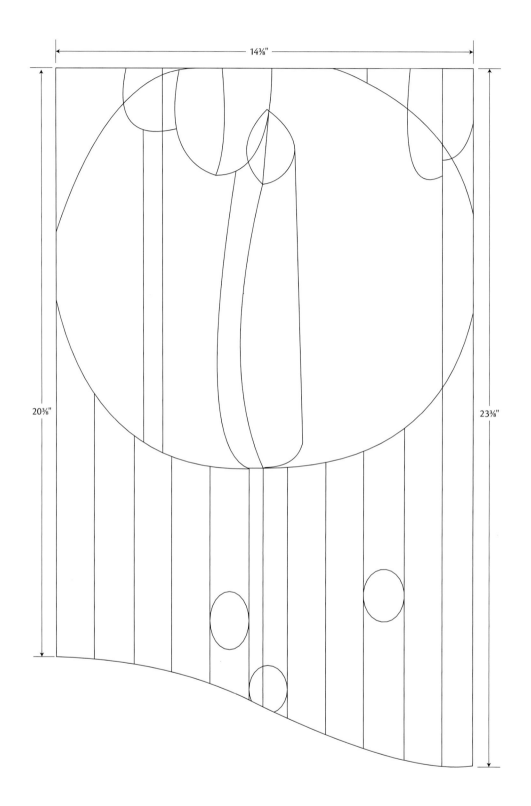

14⅜"

20⅜"

23⅜"

RIGHT SIDE GLASS PANEL DETAIL

# DIRECTOR'S ROOM ARMCHAIR

31¾" high x 21¼" wide x 18⅞" deep
(1904), stained oak

I N 1904, MACKINTOSH produced a series of designs for the Director's Room of the Glasgow School of Art, including high-backed chairs, a conference table and this low-backed armchair. It is reminiscent of the hall chairs produced for Hill House, although the back of this chair terminates well above the seat instead of extending below it. The seat is upholstered with cloth rather than reed. Alexander Martin built 12 of them at a price of £1.18 ($146) per chair.

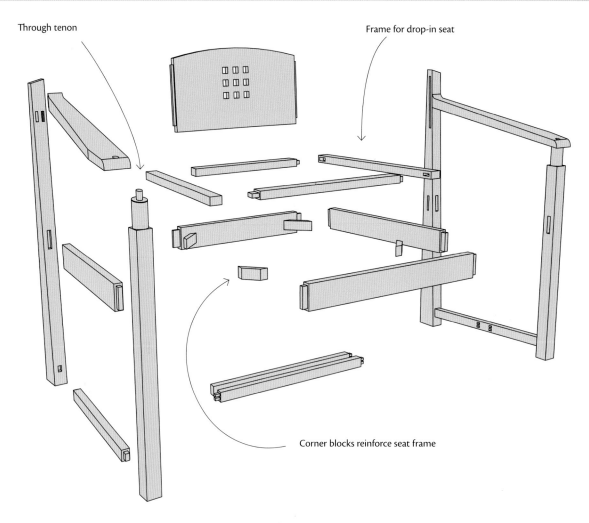

Through tenon

Frame for drop-in seat

Corner blocks reinforce seat frame

**EXPLODED VIEW**

# DIRECTOR'S ROOM ARM CHAIR

| QUANTITY | DESCRIPTION | THICKNESS | WIDTH | LENGTH | COMMENTS |
|---|---|---|---|---|---|
| 2 | Front legs | 1⅜" | 1⅜" | 24¹¹⁄₃₂" | ⅝" tenon top end |
| 2 | Back legs | 1⅜" | 2⅜" | 30⅞" | |
| 1 | Back stretcher | ¾" | 2¼" | 16⅛" | ¾" TBE* |
| 1 | Bottom back stretcher** | ¾" | 1" | 18" | ½" double TBE* |
| 1 | Bottom front stretcher** | ¾" | 1" | 18¹⁵⁄₃₂" | ½" double TBE* |
| 2 | Bottom side stretchers) | 1" | 2¹¹⁄₁₆" | 16¼" | ½" TBE* |
| 1 | Front stretcher | ¾" | 2¼" | 19½" | ½" TBE* |
| 2 | Side stretchers | 2¼" | 2¹¹⁄₁₆" | 17⁵⁄₆₄" | ½" TBE* |
| 1 | Back | ¾" | 8" | 15⅛" | ¼" TBE* |
| 2 | Arms | 3¹⁵⁄₁₆" | 4¹⁹⁄₃₂" | 18²²⁄₃₂" | ¾" double tenon back end |
| 2 | Front corner blocks | 1" | 1¹⁵⁄₁₆" | 2¹⁄₁₆" | |
| 2 | Rear corner blocks | 1" | 2⁹⁄₆₄" | 2⁵⁄₁₆" | |
| 1 | Seat frame front cleat*** | ¾" | 1¼" | 16⅛" | |
| 2 | Seat frame side cleats*** | ¾" | 3⁹⁄₆₄" | 16⅛" | |
| 1 | Seat frame rear cleat*** | ¾" | 1¼" | 12½" | |

*Tenon both ends

**Stretchers are beveled as the chair tapers from front to back.

***Seat frame cleats are glued & screwed to chair aprons.

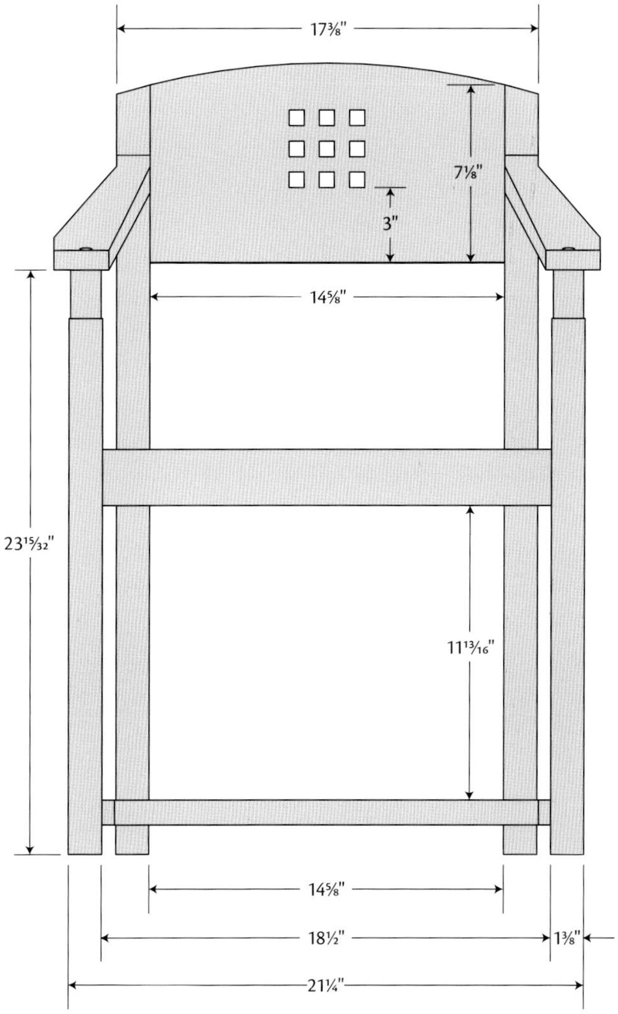
17⅜"
7⅛"
3"
14⅝"
23¹⁵⁄₃₂"
11¹³⁄₁₆"
14⅝"
18½"
1⅜"
21¼"

ELEVATION

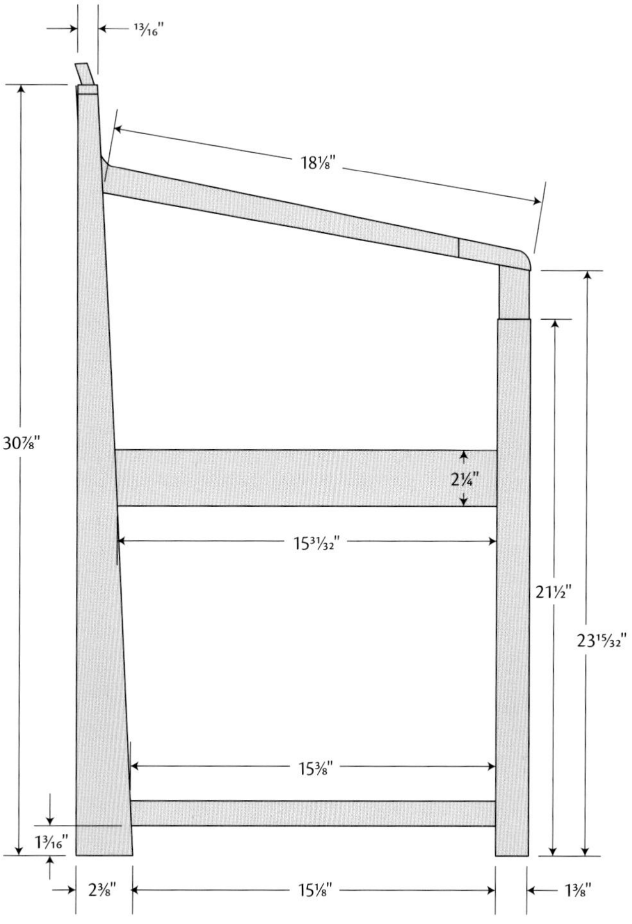
¹³⁄₁₆"
18⅛"
30⅞"
2¼"
15³¹⁄₃₂"
21½"
23¹⁵⁄₃₂"
15⅜"
1³⁄₁₆"
2⅜"
15⅛"
1⅜"

PROFILE

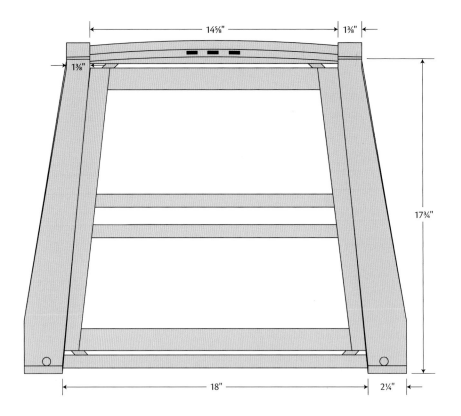

PLAN

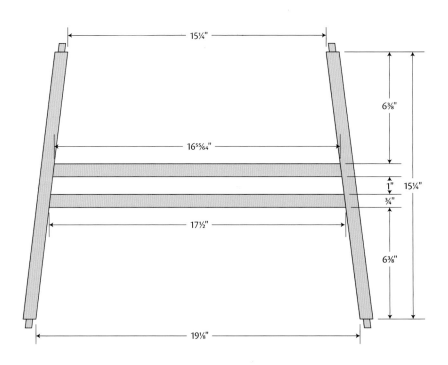

STRETCHER ASSEMBLY DETAIL PLAN VIEW

# HOUS'HILL SECRETARY

45" high x 30" wide x 12" deep
(1904)

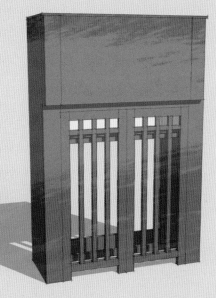

A FALL-FRONT DESKTOP is supported by gatelegs in this secretary Mackintosh designed for the Blue Bedroom at Hous'hill. The minimalist design seems subdued compared to the washstand Mackintosh designed for the same space (see page 62). The austere front is lightened by inset purple art glass (a purple echoed in the handles of the washstand). When lowered, the top reveals an abstract rose design executed in metal and glass framed by the pigeonhole dividers. Francis Smith was paid £4.33 ($555) for the case, McCulloch £4 ($513) for the glasswork.

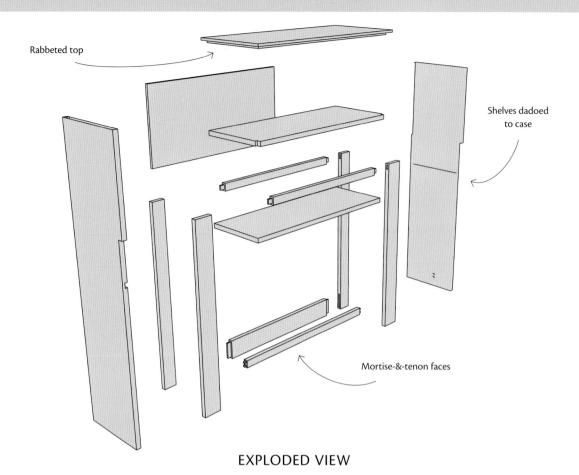

Rabbeted top

Shelves dadoed
to case

Mortise-&-tenon faces

**EXPLODED VIEW**

## HOUS'HILL SECRETARY

| QUANTITY | DESCRIPTION | THICKNESS | WIDTH | LENGTH | COMMENTS |
|---|---|---|---|---|---|
| 2 | Sides | ¾" | 12" | 44⅝" | |
| 1 | Top | ¾" | 12¾" | 30" | ¾" rabbet all around |
| **Base** | | | | | |
| 1 | Back bottom rail | ¾" | 3¼" | 25½" | ¾" TBE* |
| 2 | Front/back aprons | ¾" | 1¼" | 25½" | ¾" TBE* |
| 1 | Shelf | ¾" | 10½" | 29¼" | |
| 1 | Bottom stretcher | ¾" | 1¼" | 29¼" | ⅜" double TBE* |
| 6 | Gate inner stiles | ¾" | ¾" | 26½" | ¾" TBE*; rabbeted for inlay square |
| 2 | Gate lower rails | ¾" | 1¼" | 10½" | ¾" TBE* |
| 2 | Gate middle rails | ¾" | ¾" | 10½" | ¾" TBE*; rabbeted for inlay square |
| 4 | Gate stiles | ¾" | 1½" | 29¼" | |
| 2 | Gate upper rails | ¾" | 1½" | 10½" | ¾" TBE*; rabbeted for inlay square |
| 8 | Inlay squares | ⅛" | 1¹⁵⁄₁₆" | 1¹⁵⁄₁₆" | |
| 4 | Leg facings | ¾" | 3" | 30½" | |
| **Top** | | | | | |
| 1 | Case back | ½" | 14⅛" | 29¼" | |
| 2 | Door breadboard ends | ¾" | 2⅝" | 14⅛" | |
| 1 | Door panel | ¾" | 14⅛" | 25" | ½" TBE* |
| 1 | Pigeonhole long horizontal divider | ¼" | 8" | 12⅛" | |
| 4 | Pigeonhole short horizontal dividers | ¼" | 3⅞" | 8" | |
| 4 | Pigeonhole short vertical dividers | ¼" | 8" | 8½" | |
| 2 | Pigeonhole top and bottoms | ¼" | 8" | 28½" | |
| 6 | Pigeonhole vertical dividers | ¼" | 8" | 12¾" | |
| 1 | Shelf | ¾" | 11½" | 29¼" | Front corners notched for sides |

\* Tenon both ends

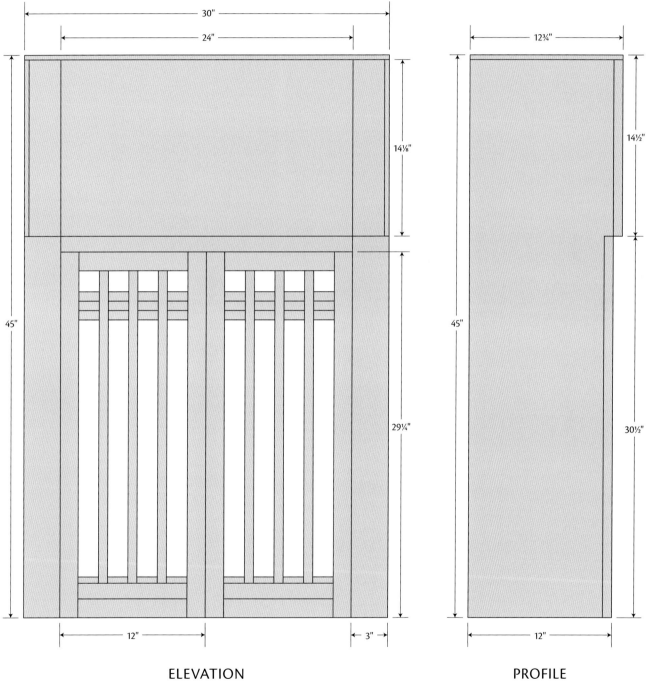

30"

24"

14⅛"

45"

29¼"

12"

3"

ELEVATION

12¾"

14½"

45"

30½"

12"

PROFILE

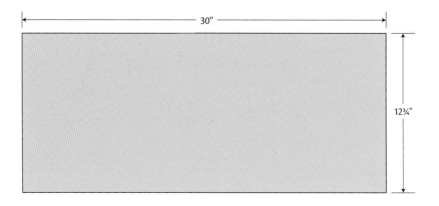

30"

12¾"

TOP

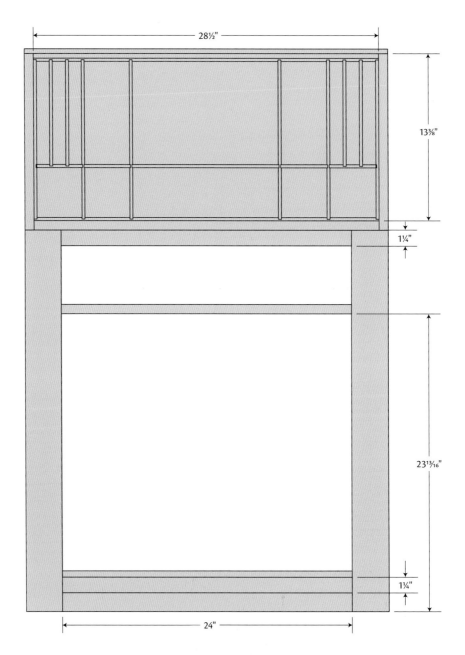

28½"

13⅜"

1¼"

23¹³⁄₁₆"

1¼"

24"

ELEVATION (DROP FRONT &
GATE LEGS REMOVED)

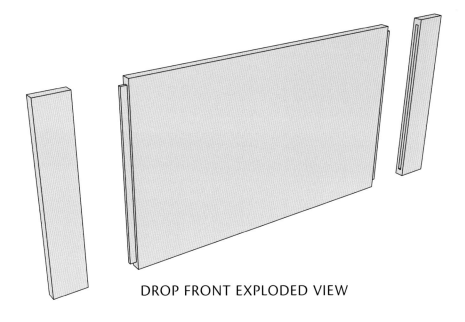

DROP FRONT EXPLODED VIEW

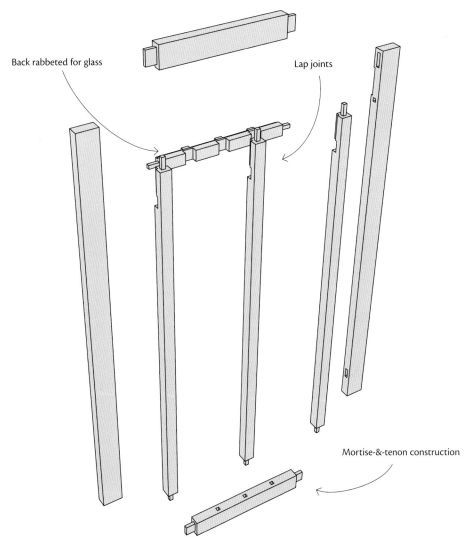

Back rabbeted for glass

Lap joints

Mortise-&-tenon construction

GATELEG EXPLODED VIEW

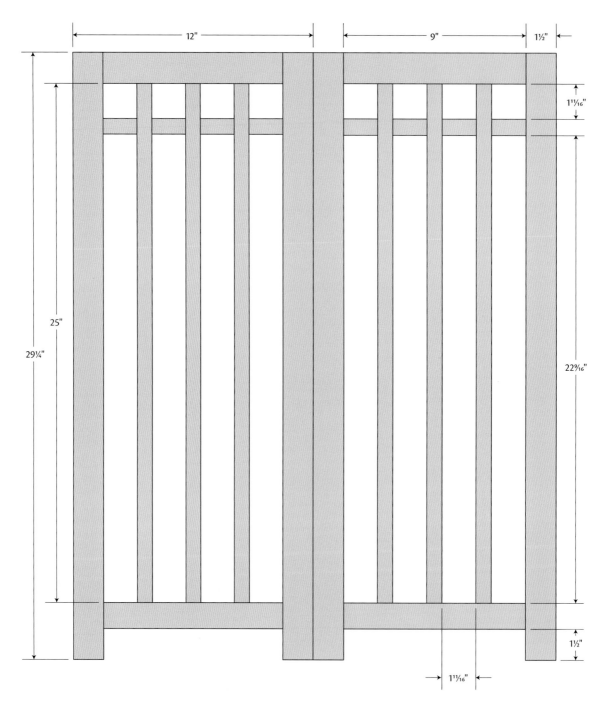

GATELEG ELEVATION

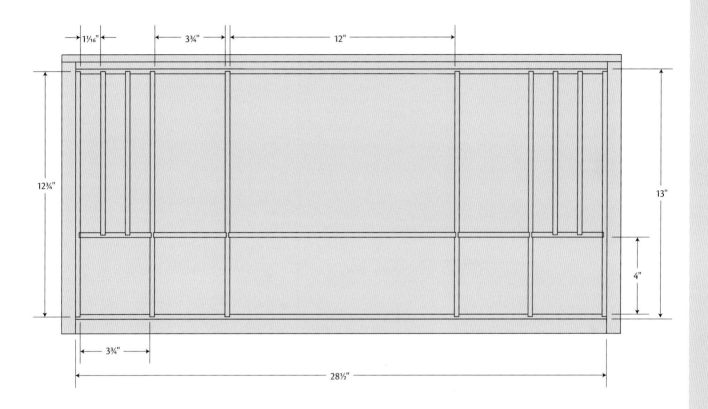

PIGEONHOLE ELEVATION

# HILL HOUSE WRITING TABLE

30" high x 24" wide x 24" deep
(1903), oak, painted white

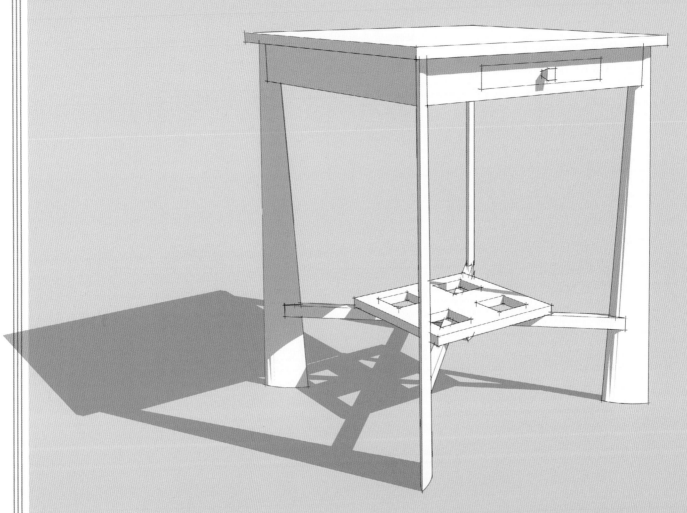

MACKINTOSH PRODUCED another variation on a table with legs set at 45° to the top with this design for the master bedroom of Hill House. Here the legs are tapered and shaped, so the apron and stretcher ends need to be scribed to accommodate their curved surfaces. The crossed stretchers support a square shelf pierced by four square cutouts. Alexander Martin was paid £4.50 ($575) to produce the table.

To simplify construction (while also aligning with other variations Mackintosh designed), preserve the flat faces of the legs while rounding over their edges. A simple miter cut is then all that's required to bring the apron and stretcher ends flush with the faces of the legs. The same basic design can be modified to produce a larger desk by sizing the top to suit, then altering the location of the legs and stretchers to match. If a rectangular top is used, the stretchers will no longer meet at 90°. The stretchers can be eliminated altogether to make more room for a chair under the table.

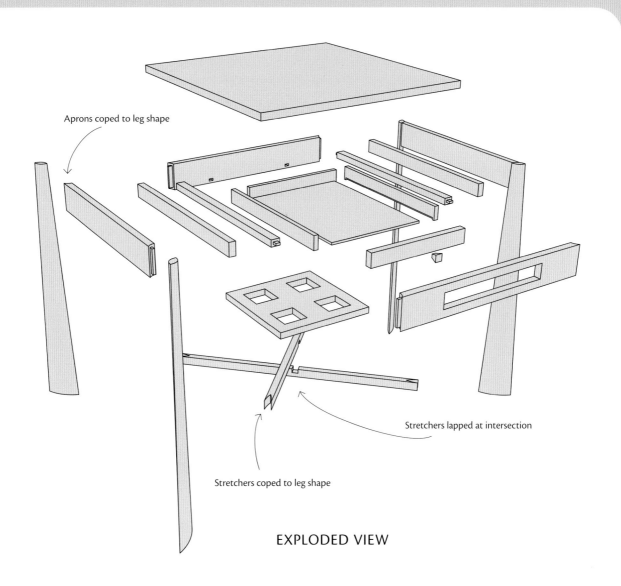

Aprons coped to leg shape

Stretchers lapped at intersection

Stretchers coped to leg shape

EXPLODED VIEW

# HILL HOUSE WRITING TABLE

| QUANTITY | DESCRIPTION | THICKNESS | WIDTH | LENGTH | COMMENTS |
|---|---|---|---|---|---|
| 4 | Legs | ¾" | 4" | 29¼" | |
| 3 | Side & back aprons | ¾" | 3" | 21" | Coped & tenoned to legs |
| 1 | Front apron | ¾" | 3" | 21" | Coped & tenoned to legs; drawer cutout |
| 2 | Stretchers | ¾" | 1" | 29⅜" | |
| 1 | Top | ¾" | 24" | 24" | |
| 1 | Shelf | ¾" | 12" | 12" | |
| 2 | Drawer rails | ¾" | 1" | 21⅜" | ½" TBE* |
| 2 | Drawer guides | ¾" | 1½" | 20⅜" | |
| 1 | Drawer front | ¾" | 1½" | 11½" | Rabbeted for drawer bottom |
| 1 | Drawer back | ½" | 1½" | 11½" | Rabbeted for drawer bottom |
| 2 | Drawer sides | ½" | 1½" | 15¾" | Rabbeted for drawer bottom |
| 1 | Drawer bottom | ¼" | 11" | 15¼" | |

Additional materials: 1 drawer pull (see Hardware Resources, page 25)

*Tenon both ends

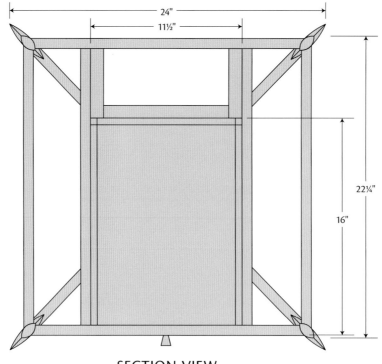

## SECTION VIEW

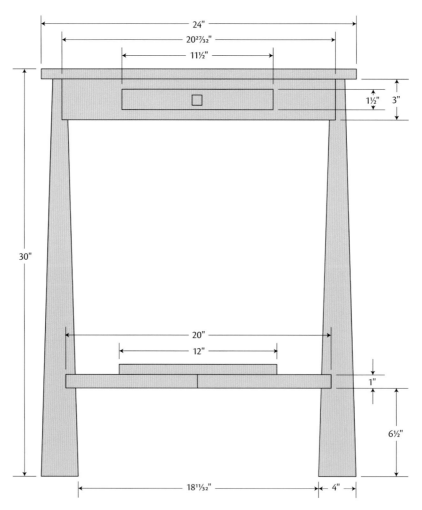

## ELEVATION

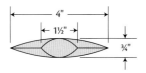

**LEG PLAN VIEW**

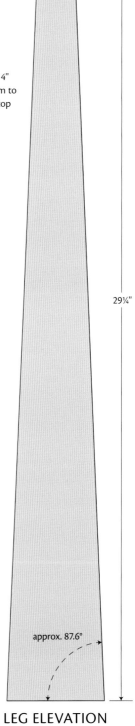

Leg tapers from 4"
wide at the bottom to
1½" wide at the top

29¼"

approx. 87.6°

**LEG ELEVATION**

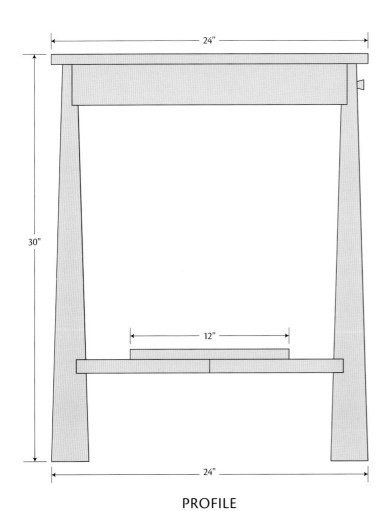

24"

30"

12"

24"

**PROFILE**

# FURTHER READING

## BEYOND THE BOOK

There's a variety of material I couldn't include in the book either due to licensing restrictions or space constraints. To provide this content to readers, I've built a support page on my website, 1910craftsman.com. For links to public domain books, images and more, visit http://www.1910craftsman.com/mackintosh-furniture.

## WORKS CONSULTED

The following resources were invaluable during my research for this book. Roger Billcliffe's "Charles Rennie Mackintosh: The Complete Furniture, Furniture Drawings, and Interior Designs" was especially helpful. For anyone interested in reading more about Mackintosh's furniture, it is the place to begin.

Agnoletti, Fernando. "The Hill House Helensburgh Erbaut von Architekt Charles Rennie Mackintosh." Deutsche Kunst und Dekoration VI (1905). 337-368. Print.

"Ein Mackintosh Tee-Haus In Glasgow." Dekorative Kunst VIII (1905)1905: 257-275. Print.

Arts & Crafts Exhibition Society. Catalogue of the Fifth Exhibition. London, Cheswick Press, 1896. Print.

Billcliffe, Roger. Mackintosh Furniture. New York: E. P. Dutton, 1984. Print.

"Charles Rennie Mackintosh: The Complete Furniture, Furniture Drawings, and Interior Designs." New York: Harry M. Abrams, 2010. Print.

"Charles Rennie Mackintosh: Textile Designs." Rohnert Park, CA: Pomegranate Artbooks, 1993. Print.

Brooker, Graeme. "Key Interiors Since 1900." London: Laurence King Publishing, 2013. Print.

Chisaburo, Yamada, ed. "Japonisme in Art: an International Symposium." Tokyo: Kodansha, 2001. Print.

Fred, W. "Die Turiner Ausstellung: Die Sektionen Schottland." Dekorative Kunst 10 (1902): 400-406. Print.

Holmes, Charles, ed. "Modern British Domestic Architecture and Decoration." New York: Offices of "The Studio", 1901. Print.

Kaplan, Wendy, ed. "Charles Rennie Mackintosh." New York: Abbeville Press, 1996. Print.

Mackintosh, Charles Rennie. "Wareham and Its Churches." The British Architect. 44 8 November (1895): 326-327. Print.

Marriott, Charles. "Modern English Architecture." London: Chapman & Hall, 1924. Print.

Muthesius, Hermann. "Die Glasgower Kunstbewegnung: Charles R. Mackintosh und Margaret Macdonald-Mackintosh." Dekorative Kunst IX (1902): 193-221. Print.

McKean, John. "Charles Rennie Mackintosh: Architect, Artist, Icon." Stillwater, MN: 2000. Print.

"The Many Colours of Mackintosh" The Scotsman 08 July 2005: n.p. Web. 13 November 2015.

"Rennie Mackintosh Locked Up as 'German Spy'." The Scotsman 29 June 2004: n.p. Web. 13 November 2015.

Robertson, Pamela, ed. "Charles Rennie Mackintosh: The Architectural Papers." Cambridge, MA: MIT Press, 1990. Print.

Sharples, Joseph. "The Architectural Career of C. R. Mackintosh." Mackintosh Architecture. University of Glasgow, n.d. Web. 21 November 2016.

"Studio Talk" The Studio. 19 (1900): 48-56. Print.

"The Studio Yearbook of Decorative Art 1907."London: Offices of the Studio, 1907. Print.

Taylor, J. "Modern Decorative Art at Glasgow." The International Studio. 30 (1907): 31-36. Print.

Wilhide, Elizabeth. "The Mackintosh Style." San Francisco: Chronicle Books, 1995. Print.

Woodman, Ellis. "Charles Rennie Mackintosh: 'Glasgow's Own Architectural Genius" The Telegraph 1 March 2015: n.p. Web. 13 November 2016.

## FURNITURE CONSTRUCTION & FINISHING

New woodworkers will find the following sources helpful as they build their skills.

I Can Do That. Collects *Popular Woodworking Magazine* articles designed to introduce new woodworkers to the craft. They also publish a manual of a basic tool set and project videos. Available for free at popularwoodworking. com/projects/icandothat

Jewitt, Jeffrey. "The Complete Illustrated Guide to Finishing." Taunton, 2004. A useful introduction to applying a range of finishes.

Lang, Robert. "Composing With Wood Grain." *Woodworking Magazine* Spring (2009): 18-23. A thorough primer on wood selection.

Rae, Andy. "The Complete Illustrated Guide to Furniture and Cabinet Construction." Taunton, 2001. Introduces standard construction techniques.

Rogowski, Gary. "The Complete Illustrated Guide to Joinery." Taunton, 2002. A comprehensive survey of cutting joints using hand and power tools.

Rodel, Kevin. "Fuming With Ammonia." Fine Woodworking 126 (1997): 46-49. Provides a concise introduction to using ammonia to color wood.

## ONLINE RESOURCES

An image search via any of the major internet search engines is a great way to see more of the buildings and furniture Mackintosh designed, but the following sites are also good launching points.

The University of Glasgow's Hunterian Museum and Art Gallery's online Mackintosh Catalogue surfaces the museum's extensive Mackintosh archives. Architectural drawings, furniture designs, and watercolors are included in the holdings: http://www.huntsearch.gla.ac.uk/Mackintosh/index.html

The former home of Bassett-Lowke is now a museum. While its focus is understandably limited, it does offer a fantastic virtual tour of the building: 78derngate.org.uk

The Charles Rennie Mackintosh Society's website provides a helpful overview of the architect's life and work in the context of Glasgow: crmsociety.com

Charles Rennie Mackintosh In Roussillon focuses on Mackintosh's life in France as a watercolorist. The site offers convenient place to view the bulk of the artist's later landscapes and presents photographs of the same locations so that visitors can see how Mackintosh manipulated the terrain to suit his artistic vision: crmackintoshfrance.com

# DEDICATION

To the memory of Richard H. Osberg. He taught me the pleasures of Chaucer, the flexibility of a navy blazer and the utility of a 1:1:1 boiled linseed oil, beeswax, turpentine mix.

# ACKNOWLEDGMENTS

My sincerest thanks to the following people:

As always, my wife Katherine provided a critical eye and patient ear.

My son Peter provided the impetus for writing these books when I sought a way to stay connected to the craft that wouldn't wake a sleeping infant with screaming power tools.

The genesis of this book was a random gift. One morning I found a copy of Roger Billcliffe's Mackintosh Furniture in my mail box. My neighbor Ben had come across it and thought I might like it. I did, and the seed of this project was planted.

The editorial staff at Popular Woodworking Books did much hard work in transforming a motley collection of images, illustrations, and text into a coherent, appealing whole.

## ABOUT THE AUTHOR

MICHAEL CROW is the author of "Mid-Century Modern Furniture" and "Building Classic Arts & Crafts Furniture: Shop Drawings for 33 Traditional Charles Limbert Projects" and a contributor to woodworking and homebuilding magazines. He can often be found working on his Craftsman bungalow or building furniture for it. Follow his work at www.1910craftsman.com.

**Mackintosh Furniture.** Copyright © 2017 by Michael Crow. Printed and bound in China. All rights reserved. No part of this book may be reproduced in any form or by any electronic or mechanical means including information storage and retrieval systems without permission in writing from the publisher, except by a reviewer, who may quote brief passages in a review. Published by Popular Woodworking Books, an imprint of F+W Media, Inc., 10151 Carver Rd. Blue Ash, Ohio, 45242. First edition.

Distributed in Canada by Fraser Direct
100 Armstrong Avenue
Georgetown, Ontario L7G 5S4
Canada

Distributed in the U.K. and Europe by
F&W Media International
Pynes Hill Court
Pynes Hill
Rydon Lane
Exeter
EX2 5AZ
United Kingdom
Tel: (+44) 1392 797680

Visit our website at popularwoodworking.com or our consumer website at shopwoodworking.com for more woodworking information.

Other fine Popular Woodworking Books are available from your local bookstore or direct from the publisher.

ISBN-13: 978-1-4403-4879-2

21  20  19  18  17      5  4  3  2  1

Editor: *Scott Francis*
Designer: *Daniel T. Pessell*
Production Coordinator: *Debbie Thomas*

a content + ecommerce company

## Metric Conversion Chart

| | | |
|---|---|---|
| Inches | Centimeters | 2.54 |
| Centimeters | Inches | 0.4 |
| Feet | Centimeters | 30.5 |
| Centimeters | Feet | 0.03 |
| Yards | Meters | 0.9 |
| Meters | Yards | 1.1 |

# Ideas ▪ Instruction ▪ Inspiration

Get downloadable woodworking instruction when you sign up
for our free newsletter at **popularwoodworking.com**.

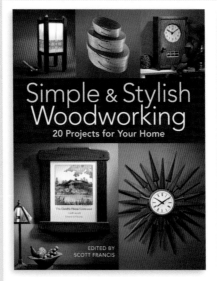

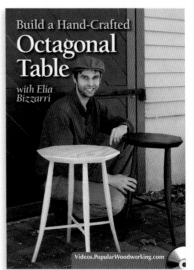

Visit **popularwoodworking.com** to subcribe (look for the red "Subscribe" button on the navigation bar).

These and other great Popular Woodworking products are available at your local bookstore, woodworking store or online supplier. Visit our website at **shopwoodworking.com**.

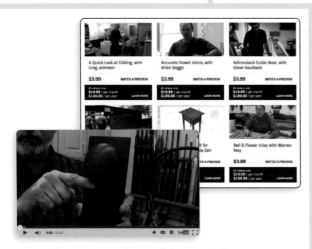

## Popular Woodworking Videos

Subscribe and get immediate access to the web's best woodworking subscription site. You'll find more than 400 hours of woodworking video tutorials and full-length video workshops from world-class instructors on workshops, projects, SketchUp, tools, techniques and more!

**videos.popularwoodworking.com**

## Visit our Website

Find helpful and inspiring articles, videos, blogs, projects and plans at **popularwoodworking.com**.

For behind the scenes information, become a fan at **Facebook.com/ popularwoodworking**

For more tips, clips and articles, follow us at **twitter.com/pweditors**

For visual inspiration, follow us at **pinterest.com/popwoodworking**

For free videos visit **youtube.com/popularwoodworking**

Follow us on Instagram **@popularwoodworking**